BIBLE
PROPHECY

BIBLE PROPHECY

Questions and Answers

Paul Erb
Introduction by
Myron S. Augsburger

HERALD PRESS
Scottdale, Pennsylvania
Kitchener, Ontario
1978

Library of Congress Cataloging in Publication Data

Erb, Paul, 1894-
  Bible prophecy.

  Bibliography: p.
  Includes index.
  1. Bible—Prophecies—Miscellanea. 2. Eschatology—
Miscellanea. I. Title.
BS647.2.E7   220.1'5   77-17597
ISBN 0-8361-1841-3

BIBLE PROPHECY: QUESTIONS AND ANSWERS
Copyright © 1978 by Herald Press, Scottdale, Pa. 15683
  Published simultaneously in Canada by Herald Press,
  Kitchener, Ont. N2G 4M5
Library of Congress Catalog Card Number: 77-17597
International Standard Book Number: 0-8361-1841-3
Printed in the United States of America
Design: Alice B. Shetler

10 9 8 7 6 5 4 3 2 1

*I dedicate
this summary of biblical prophecy
to my dear brother, Allen, now
gone to be with the Lord, whom
he deeply loved and faithfully
served. Allen was a lifelong student
of prophetic truth, and gave me much
help. He is now where he knows the
answers to questions that we asked
each other as we studied
the Scriptures.*

CONTENTS

II. The Place of Christ in Prophecy

III. Promise and Assurance in Salvation History

IV. The Church in God's Plan

V. The Kingdom of Christ

VI. The Coming of Christ

VII. The Hope of the Resurrection

VIII. The Ultimate Judgment

PREFACE

Why another book on biblical prophecy? Dozens of them have been written in the past twenty years.

This book does not tell you that Christ will come in this generation. We can't know that.

It doesn't draw a vivid imaginative picture of the "rapture." That word is not in the Bible, neither Greek nor English.

It does not argue that the present nation of Israel is a proof of a Jewish millennium, or that people will be saved during a "tribulation period," or that any specific person has been or is the antichrist, or that for the believer the judgment is past.

This book, however, will help you to see redemption as a drama, with a beginning and a climax (both in the past), and an end (in the future).

It describes the second coming of Christ as the completion of what was begun in Christ's first coming.

It shows all biblical prophecy as centering in the person and work of Christ.

It finds the certainty of what God will yet do in the certainty of what He already has done.

It expects the fullness of redemption in the resurrection of the body and the freedom of the created order.

It asserts that Christ's resurrection doomed Satan to defeat.

It uses the whole Bible to tell the whole story of the

divine age, but it lets the New Testament serve as the interpreter of the Old Testament.

It makes the how and when of prophecy less important than the who and the why.

It warns with the certainty of God's judgment, and comforts with the hope of His final salvation.

In writing this book I elaborate on the same assumptions of prophetic truth and divine revelation which I set forth in my earlier book, *The Alpha and the Omega.*

To make for easy reading, I have used a simple style and a clearly defined vocabulary. Sources, where deemed necessary, are indicated in the text without footnotes. Biblical quotes are from the American Standard Version (1901), except where otherwise noted.

I am grateful to Herald Press for permission to draw extensively from *The Alpha and the Omega* (1955, now out of print). I acknowledge my indebtedness to other recent authors and publishers listed in the bibliography, especially to George E. Ladd for his excellent treatment, *A Theology of the New Testament.*

I thank Dr. Myron S. Augsburger for his help in formulating the questions, in answering Nos. 3, 12, 14, and 44, in his critical reading of my answers, and for writing the introduction.

Special thanks to my wife, Alta Mae Erb, for listening with a critical ear, and to Paul M. Schrock, editor of Herald Press, for planning and affirming.

I pray that this book may build a stronger faith in the prophecy of the Bible, and warn against going beyond biblical revelation to gain a hearing by speculation.

Paul Erb
Scottdale, Pennsylvania

INTRODUCTION

The second coming of Jesus Christ is an essential part of the Christian message. His return will bring about the culmination of history as we know it, and "time shall be no more." History will end neither with a whimper nor with a bang, but with the glorious consummation of the purpose of God in Jesus Christ. This is what Jürgen Moltmann, the German theologian, describes as a *Theology of Hope.*

It is important that we emphasize the birth-death-rising again of Jesus Christ as the high point or the climax of history. The incarnation is final in God's revelation. Christ's resurrection marked the ultimate victory over sin, Satan, and death. We now enjoy the privilege of victory as we appropriate the lordship of Jesus Christ in our lives. In this victory the Christian already lives in the light of the second coming. He lives as a part of the *eschaton,* that is, the influence in the present of our assurance of the ultimate culmination of history in the return of Christ. His second coming will usher us into the ultimate state of being in the presence of God, that for which man was created and for which God's redemptive program has been negotiated. According to Paul in Romans 8, we are saved by this hope, by the absolute assurance that the victory which Jesus Christ accomplished on Calvary will eventually be expressed in the total of creation.

Throughout church history there has been much speculation regarding the signs of the end and the return of Jesus Christ. But Jesus left the timing with the Father and said to us, "Occupy till I come" (KJV). The most authentic word one can express regarding the nearness of Christ's return is stated by the Apostle Paul, "For now is salvation nearer to us than when we first believed" (Romans 13:11). On the other hand, for those who claimed that the meaning of the second coming was already fulfilled by the work of the Spirit in the church, the Apostle Paul explicitly told the Thessalonians that the day of the Lord will not come until that man of sin is revealed (2 Thessalonians 2:3).

Jesus told us, "As were the days of Noah, so shall be the coming of the Son of man." The most striking thing about the day of Noah is that the impact of the preaching mission upon society had reached a stalemate. There were no converts to the people of God. Consequently, God could send a flood in judgment without being charged that if He had waited longer there would have been more converts. From this one might conclude that there will be a stalemate between the impact of the gospel and the response from society at the end of the age, making it impossible to accuse God of ending history prematurely. However, it does not appear that this stalemate is present as the Christian church continues to grow. In every continent of the world except Europe and America Christianity is growing rapidly. One quarter of the world's population of 4 billion people profess the Christian faith, an all-time high in Christian history. This is a part of what Jesus meant when He said the gospel shall be carried into all the world and then the end shall come.

On the other hand, the human dilemma of man's sinfulness continues to be expressed in moral perversions, ecological disorders, economic exploitations, violence, and lack of compassionate relationships. It appears that God may allow humanity to so tie itself into knots that there is no way out. When mankind has so completely perverted its own order of history that there is no possible correction, then God can end it all and usher in a new age without unbelievers accusing Him of lacking mercy or being unduly impatient. This perspective affirms that God's judgments, as well as His redemption, are being worked out in history. We can read something of the times and the fulfillment of prophecy in the human predicament itself.

Of what benefit is the study of prophecy? We study prophecy to watch the footsteps of God in history, to understand the providence of God at work today, to interpret our times, and to avoid being caught up in secularism, materialism, and general humanism. And above all, we study prophecy to affirm our faith in the ultimate purpose of God for humanity and the transcendent meaning of His victory. As we read the happenings in society, the happenings among the nations, and the happenings with the people of Israel (the people which Barth calls "God's living sermon to the world"), we are better able to relate to our times as pilgrims who have no continuing city here.

God is not capricious. Because God is consistent with Himself, the prophecies and fulfillments recorded in the Bible enable us to understand prophecies and the fulfillments that are yet to come.

This book by Paul Erb is an important contribution to the Christian church in our reflections on prophecy. I do not know any other quite like it. It raises questions and provides insight and understanding regardless of one's particular prophetic persuasion. It proposes considerations without being dogmatic, and offers guidance with a humility which does not claim to have the final answers to all questions.

Revealing a breadth of insight in terms of prophetic views and perspectives, Brother Erb maintains a consistent pattern of refraining from dogmatism, a stance which is especially appropriate in light of Jesus' words in Acts 1, "It is not for you to know times or seasons, which the Father hath set within his own authority. But ye shall receive power, when the Holy Spirit is come upon you: and ye shall be my witness both in Jerusalem, and in all Judaea and Samaria, and unto the uttermost part of the earth."

It is my prayer that this book may help the Christian church become more positive and aggressive in sharing the good news of the gospel throughout the world.

Myron S. Augsburger
Harrisonburg, Virginia

1

The Meaning of Prophecy

1. Is prophecy the foretelling of future events?

For most people prophecy means telling about a happening before it occurs. A prophet for them is a person who is able to predict. A weather prophet, for example, is one who tries to tell us today what the weather will be like tomorrow. A political prophet declares who the next president will be.

A related idea is that a prophet is one who is ahead of his time. An article in a church paper, for instance, says that Frederick Douglass, the freed slave who spoke against slavery before the Civil War, was a prophetic voice.

Likewise, most people assume that biblical prophecy foretells future events. Old Testament prophecy, they think, foretells the first coming of Christ, and what happened then. And New Testament prophecy foretells the second coming of Christ and related developments, such as the resurrection and the judgment.

But a prophet in the Bible is one who speaks forth in behalf of another. Peter says, "No prophecy ever came by the will of man: but men spake from God, being moved by the Holy Spirit" (2 Peter 1:21). A prophet was God's spokesman, and prophecy, in a broad sense, was the message of the prophet, whatever he felt led to communicate.

What does God have to say to mankind? Not primarily the announcement of future events. God wants persons to do His holy will. And so the chief message of His prophet is to tell what that will is. A true prophet decries anything that is against divine holiness, and encourages anything that is for it. He describes the good results of obedience to God. The goal of prophecy is the holiness of God, experienced by mankind in and beyond history.

So the prophet is primarily a spokesman for God. This has been called forthtelling. But speaking for God includes also foretelling. For God wants man to know the future. He announces through the prophet that He will send a Redeemer from sin. He has a great future for those who accept this Redeemer. And He tells of tragic consequences for those who reject the Savior.

The heart of prophecy is Jesus Christ. Prophecy is about Him: His first coming to accomplish redemption, and His second coming to bring redemption's history to its consummation.

Yes, prophecy includes a large element of prediction. Both the Old Testament and the New predict what God will do. However, God through His prophets tells us not simply what will happen, but why. In the biblical sense, prophets are both forthtellers of righteousness and foretellers of the future.

2. Where can we find answers to our questions about the future?

All of us have questions about the future. Are there answers for these questions? Where can they be found?

It is ordinarily assumed that we cannot know anything for certain about the future. What has happened, we can know, at least sometimes. We remember, or someone else remembers, and can tell us. There may be a written account of the event, and we can read it. Archives and libraries contain records that can be researched.

But what has not yet happened, who can know? We can reason from the past what may happen. We can make shrewd guesses as to what is coming. But know? Oh, no!

Unless God, who knows the future as well as the past, should tell us. That would be a miracle of revelation, the sort of thing that seldom happens.

But it did happen. God told prophets what He intended to do in the course of human history. The prophet or someone else wrote down what He said. It became a part of the Word of God, and predicted future events. Isaiah describes the process in 42:9, "Before they spring forth I tell you of them."

Thus before it happened the Scriptures foretold that Jerusalem would be destroyed, first by Babylon, and later by Rome; that the Messiah would be born in Bethlehem and die on a cross; that the Holy Spirit would empower the Christian believers. All these things happened as predicted. Likewise we can know that Christ will come again, that the dead shall rise again, and that the just and the unjust shall be judged. These things will happen just as predicted.

We may have questions to which God has not given the answers. Some things, such as the date of Christ's second coming, we cannot know until the event occurs. We can know some things that will happen in the future, but only as they are revealed by God's Word. Only from God, as revealed by His prophets, can we know what has not happened, but is yet to come.

3. Do the stars, the pyramids, astrology, and the visions of mystics foretell the future?

Through the centuries people have been obsessed with attempts to interpret the future. Persons have made bold claims that they have gifts of projection and insights into the future have often received widespread attention.

However, these are simply persons who have the ability to read happenings and the character of others and make reasonable projections. Many times they are right simply because of their ability to interpret personalities and understand what they will do in certain circumstances.

One good example is the case of the court jester under Louis XIV of France, who fell into disfavor and was summoned before the king. The king asked him whether he could foretell his own future. He responded, "Yes, your honor, I will die three days before your majesty does!" The king took good care of him the rest of his life.

In Daniel we read that Nebuchadnezzar dreamed a dream but had forgotten it. He wanted it recalled, together with its interpretation. He summoned all his wise men. When they could not tell him the dream, he was about to have them all executed. Daniel asked for an audience with the king and declared with confidence, "In a few days I will tell you your dream." This is an example not of a fortune-teller, but of a man with faith enough to believe that God would reveal what he needed to know.

Today astrology has become a multimillion-dollar business. People consult the stars and their horoscopes as though these were the final authority for their lives. True, the wise men of the East journeyed to Jerusalem seeking for Christ because they had seen His star and had come to worship Him. This was His star; God was giving a special revelation and it had nothing to do with interpreting a horoscope. All the way through the Bible, from the magicians of Pharaoh to the "old wives' fables" that Paul protested against, we have a clear distinction between the fatalism of astrology and the true meaning of divine providence.

Fatalism has led persons to study the pyramids in Egypt, especially the Great Pyramid near Cairo, in an attempt to find there a projection of the whole scope of history.

More subtle is the art of the fortune-teller. It is true that there are dimensions of extrasensory perception, of communication between minds, and even of the communication of events to some minds, which go beyond our full understanding. There are supernatural awarenesses which seem to be either divine or demonic. When fortune-tellers are speaking of something that is happening at some distant point, they are sometimes quite accurate. But in projecting the future, they can make only a good guess.

We should remember that only God has foreknowledge. The devil himself is limited and has to understand the unfolding of history just as we do. Because he takes God's Word seriously and knows what God's purposes are, he is aware that his own time is getting short. Without foreknowledge he cannot project all of the future. But by his power he may give persons a vision of something that is happening at some other point, and thereby make a great impression. We must beware of allowing this to cause us to waver from the will of Christ.

To walk in faith is far more satisfying than to try to have answers for everything in the future. To know all that will happen to us in the next five years would not be good for us. The knowledge of successes would ruin us, and the knowledge of failures would destroy us. Put your hand in God's, and trust Him for the future.

4. Why is the study of prophecy in danger of unbiblical speculation?

No area of theological study involves wider differences of opinion than eschatology. All of these prophecy students claim to be following the teachings of the Bible, yet their teachings are often mutually contradictory. They draw prophetic blueprints which have little similarity, and they may feel strongly about their differences. Some have contended that the "rapture" of the saints will occur at the beginning of a seven-year tribulation period. But others have insisted that the "rapture" will not take place until the end of that tribulation. And at a conference in England the two groups refused to appear on the same platform to consider their differences of opinion.

Why such differences?

On opinions which relate to the future, it is difficult to prove that one is right and another wrong. To defend what is only opinion, a person tries too hard to find arguments, and finds them in supposing or imagining. Language must be interpreted, and interpretations may get pretty wild.

Regarding future events, there are some blanks where the Bible just does not supply information for a full picture. The natural temptation is to make guesses in order to fill the blanks. One writer warns against putting false teeth into the mouth of prophecy. Where the Word is silent, blanks should remain blank.

Some interpreters hate to admit ignorance, and what may be only inferred or implied they give as clear teaching. But revelation is enough; speculation is more than enough. Ideas get built into a system, and then the logic of a system tells people what to believe.

The only prophecy which is trustworthy is that which God has spoken in His Word; speculation, prejudice, or imagination are threats to genuine prophecy.

5. Can we be certain about the fulfillment of biblical prophecy?

In spite of some differences concerning prophecy, is there firm ground to stand on? Will God actually do what He has promised to do?

The character of God is involved in those questions. Paul wrote to Titus, "In hope of eternal life, which God, who cannot lie, promised before times eternal" (1:2). That's the kind of God He is! What He promises, He is able to perform. And He would not have promised what He did not want to do.

Writing to the Romans about the faith of Abraham, Paul said the patriarch did not hesitate to take God at His word, "being fully assured that what he had promised, he was able also to perform" (4:21). Abraham's "absolute certainty" (Weymouth) came from his acquaintance with God. The promise was as good as the One who promised. It always has been, and it still is. The author of Hebrews said, "He is faithful that promised" (10:23).

We can believe that prophetic promises will be fulfilled because some of them have already been fulfilled. The process of fulfillment has already begun, and it only needs to be continued. One sees the fulfillment in the Old Testament story of God's people, like when many of them returned to Jerusalem, as Jeremiah had prophesied seventy years earlier.

Many prophecies were turned into history at the first coming of Christ. The New Testament describes this great concentration of fulfillment. Thus was the word of the prophet fulfilled, said the Gospel writers. If we accept the Gospels as true, then we do not question whether prophecy is fulfilled.

So likewise with the prophecies about Christ that have not yet been fulfilled. We are sure they will be fulfilled as a continuation of what has been fulfilled in the past. We are not just waiting for the "last things" to happen. The "last things" are even now in process.

Ours is the gospel of promise. The word "promise" is found almost forty times in the New Testament. The only condition on the promise is the real meaning of that promise. There is certainty wherever the meaning of revelation is clear. That meaning is what the prophecy actually says, not the meaning that we may read into it. It must be in harmony with Christ, the living center of the Word.

Let us admit that there are problems in understanding the language of prophecy. There are things that must be interpreted as figures of speech. For example, Isaiah says that "every hill shall be made low." No one supposes that this predicts a gigantic bulldozing job. Some may go too far in fitting a prophecy into current events. An example would be making Ezekiel 38 and 39 a prediction concerning the Russia of our decades. Or the ten kings of Revelation 17:12—that they are the ten nations of the Common Market in Europe (assuming that the tenth nation will join the nine now—1976—in the Common Market).

Throughout the Christian era it has been a fault of interpretation to suppose that the prophetic word is about the happenings of the present date. When the date passes, and some other fulfillment for the prophecy must be found, people begin to wonder about the certainty of prophetic fulfillment.

We must be humble enough to admit that we do not know just how to expect prophecy to become history. In fact, we do not need to know all the answers. We must let predictive problems wait for their solutions.

Prophecy often pictures details of the eternal world. And it is difficult for the children of time to comprehend the things of the eternal. Karl Heim says this is like children trying to participate in the conversation of adults.

So the certainty of the fulfillment is conditioned by how clear the prediction is, and how effective is its interpretation.

We do not know everything, or even much, about the future. But we do know enough to give us an adequate warning and a certain hope.

God is not capricious, and the way He has acted in the past assures future action.

6. Why are there so many differences among the students of prophecy?

The Bible does tell us how God's purposes will be developed as history comes to its end. But it is not easy for Bible readers to understand that story in the same way. In fact, there are many opposing interpretations of

what is going to happen, and when, and in what se-
quences. And so the interpreters find themselves divided
into "schools" of prophecy.

For instance, how many times is Christ coming? All
schools agree in calling His birth at Bethlehem His first
coming. Some speak of the coming of the Holy Spirit at
Pentecost as a second coming, and they believe that His
promise to come again was fulfilled then or later when
the Spirit came to live in the believers.

Others are looking for Christ to come in what they
call the "rapture," to bring the church age to an end, as
He takes believers away from the earth while the rest of
the people go through a terrible tribulation period of
seven years.

At the end of these seven years, according to the
understanding of these people, Christ will come again
with His church to enter into a reign of one thousand
years on the earth.

Has Christ come the second time already? And will
He come once or twice more to bring this age to an end?

It's too bad that the argument about such matters
sometimes becomes sharp and bitter. Rightly dividing
the word of truth, it seems, may wrongly divide God's
people. Since all we have to do is determine what the Bible says, why all the differences?

For one thing, at no place in the Bible are all the
teachings on prophecy gathered together and clearly
harmonized. A variety of authors wrote far apart from
each other, and from us, in both time and place. They
wrote about events that have never yet happened, and so
are hard to visualize. They used many figures of speech
and symbols which need to be interpreted. For instance,
a sword coming from the mouth of Jesus obviously

refers to His words, not to a steel weapon. Paul says we "see through a glass darkly" (in an *enigma,* Gk.) and someday the enigma will have to be solved. The prophetic material is condensed, and often needs fuller description. It seems to be quite certain that after it is fulfilled we shall be saying, "I didn't know it would be like this."

Our pride keeps us from being good learners. We call one another "scholars," when possibly we have just quit learning. Frank Lloyd Wright once said, "An expert is a man who has stopped thinking. He knows!" When a prophecy student admits that he is less sure of some of his interpretations than he used to be, it is likely that he is making progress toward the truth.

Some Bible readers may only be trying to satisfy their curiosity, and prophecy doesn't have that purpose. We may be unwilling in our arrogance to leave some questions unanswered. And so we guess at the answers because we are unwilling to say, "I don't know."

When Peter asked Jesus what was going to happen to John, Jesus replied, "What is that to you?" When prophecy study begins to ride hobbies, it looks for evidences to bolster its point of view and accepts whatever it wants to be true. Many charts of prophetic sequence are influenced too much by the questions people ask. We must always pay more attention to the answers the Scriptures give.

7. What is eschatology?

This book is a series of questions and answers on eschatology. And what is that?

Eschatology is a big word formed from two shorter Greek ones. Why Greek? Because the New Testament was written in Greek, and eschatology is a part of New Testament studies.

The two Greek words are *eschatos* and *logos.* Logos (word) is a study or a discourse on a branch of knowledge; *theology,* for instance, is the study of God (theos).

The second word is *eschatos,* an adjective meaning *last.* In theology this word modifies *times* or *things.* And so *eschatology* is a study of end times or last events or things. There is a noun *eschaton,* which is the concern of eschatology.

The subject of eschatology is the future of man, of history, of the world. It studies what God has revealed about what is going to happen last of all: not only what, but how and when and why; by whom and to whom. It includes God's promises and plans concerning the future. It shows how those plans have developed from the beginning of time and will continue to develop to the end of time.

Without eschatology the rest of theology is incomplete. The doctrines of God, man, Christ, salvation, and the church need to be followed through to the necessary conclusion at the end of the age. In a phrase which everybody understands, the concern of eschatology is "the end of the world." But to know the end, we also need to know the beginning, and the direction of development from the beginning to the end.

Individual eschatology considers what lies ahead for each person. Many important questions involve every one of us—questions about death, life after death, what happens to our bodies, the judgment.

Then there is general eschatology—the growth of a people of God, God's plans for the church, the coming of Christ to bring history to its consummation. It is important to know these things too. And in the prophetic Scriptures God has taken us into His confidence in revealing unto us what He will do.

This revelation is what eschatology is all about.

8. Are people interested in eschatology today?

The interest in eschatology today is great and widespread. This is expressed in many ways.

Scores of new books related to this subject keep pouring from the presses. Some of them are scholarly and competent, such as *Encyclopedia of Biblical Prophecy* (Payne, 1973) and *A Theology of the New Testament* (Ladd, 1974), in which eschatology is a recurring theme. Billy Graham's *Angels* (1975), with many references to prophecy, has at this writing (1977) been for two years on the best-selling list, with total sales of considerably over a million.

A spate of books, one after the other, present a variety of apocalyptic viewpoints. The most popular has been Hal Lindsay's *The Late Great Planet Earth* (1970), with over ten million in print. Wilkerson's *The Vision* (1974) and many others have sold widely. *The Second Coming Bible* (Biederwolf, first edition in 1924 as *Millennial Bible*), is also popular. Herald Press has contributed *The Great Trek* (Belk, 1976), an account of a strange fanaticism which drew some hundreds of Russian Mennonites to meet Christ in Siberia in 1917. One book, *Guide to Survival,* with advice for people who are left behind in the "rapture," illustrates what has been called the "rapture fever."

Articles on this current interest have appeared in *Time, Newsweek,* and practically all religious magazines.

The New York Times and *Christian Science Monitor* have carried feature articles on it.

Louis Cassels in a United Press story described the excitement about the comet Kohoutek, "the Christmas star of 1973." In a tract, "The Coming Comet," Carl McIntire said, "The second coming of Christ is being announced."

Movies—"His Land," "The Return," "Road to Armageddon," and others—have helped to dramatize prophecy for thousands. Cassette recordings of prophetic sermons have spoken with conviction, even obsession—"I believe that all the events mentioned will happen in this generation."

Bumper stickers warn, "When the rapture comes this car will be driverless." One of the "Jesus people" in California, when asked whether he wanted to enter college the next fall, replied, "Jesus will come before that."

Yes, people are interested in prophecy. Not that this is a new thing. Anticipation of Christ's return has waxed and waned throughout the 2000-year history of Christianity. It was strong among the first-century Christians who faced Roman persecution. It rose to a peak around AD 1200, when readers of Revelation thought that the 1,260 days were years, and so the end was near. A similar excitement prevailed at the time of the Reformation (1500). We seem now to be in another peak of interest in the last things. It is a time for thankfulness, for joyous watching, and for caution.

9. Are we living now in the last days?

Yes, we are now in the last days, as the New Testament uses that phrase and others like it. The author of

Hebrews means his own time when he says that God "hath at the end of these days spoken unto us in his Son" (1:2); and that "at the end of the ages hath he been manifested to put away sin" (9:26).

In 1 Corinthians 10:11, Paul is writing of his own contemporaries, "upon whom the ends of the ages are come." Timothy was told to turn away, evidently in his time, from the evil men who were to come in the "last days" (2 Timothy 3:1).

Peter talks of something already past when he says Christ "was manifested at the end of the time" (1 Peter 1:20). And John says, "It is the last hour" (1 John 2:18).

Now we have come to speak of the days shortly before the second coming as the last days. And we suppose that the descriptions of mockers to come are signs of Christ's near return. Actually the end times are the whole period between the two comings of Christ. Because we do not know when Christ is coming, any present time may be near to the "last day." We have been in the latter days now for almost two thousand years, and we shall be in those days until the "last day," when Christ will come.

We cannot argue from the Scriptures that any specific year, say 1978, is very near to the "day of the Lord." We do know that we are nearer to that day than ever before. But we cannot be so sure about the "signs of the times" that we can know the end is within a month or a year, or even a century.

10. What is apocalyptic literature?

One dictionary defines apocalyptic literature as Jewish and Christian writings between 200 BC and AD 100, involving heavy use of symbolic imagery and the expectation of an imminent cosmic cataclysm in which God would destroy the ruling powers of evil and raise the righteous to life in a messianic kingdom.

In the centuries just before and after Christ, the Jewish people struggled with pessimism. They thought they had been true to God. But God had let them down. They were still a subject people. Would God reward them with victory over their enemies?

Yes, but not in this age. God, said the apocalyptics, will break into history. The eternal kingdom of God is dawning.

The apocalyptics were the writers—they were not preachers—who rewrote history to assure God's people of triumph and salvation in an age to come. They wrote about secrets of the heavenly world and the events of the end times. They were pessimistic about history—this age. They were optimistic, however, about the age to come, the messianic era.

There were many of these writers, and they produced an extensive apocalyptic literature. A few of their books were accepted into the sacred canon, including Daniel, of the Old Testament, and Revelation of the New Testament. These are a part of the Bible. Some, like Baruch and Esdras (Ezra), became a part of the Apocrypha. And others, like Enoch and Assumption of Moses, are part of what is called the Pseudepigrapha. The authors whose names these books carry, for the most part, are ancient worthies who give the books integrity and authority. Daniel, for instance, is a book not by Daniel, but about him and his experiences and visions.

The style of this literature gives it a character of its own. It abounds in dreams, visions, and angel guides, and other symbols. It is poetic, full of strange animal imagery and numerology. It speaks of truth which cannot be known except by the divine revelation which it claims. And so the last book of the New Testament bears the Greek title, Apocalypse.

This literature was well known to the Jews and the Christians of the early church. The eschatology and prophetic teachings of Jesus and the apostles were more understandable then than they are to us. We do not know the apocalyptic books because most of them did not get into the Bible. When Jesus spoke to the high priest of His coming on "the clouds of heaven", it was in a familiar expression in Jewish vocabulary.

And so apocalyptic writing is a kind of bridge between the two Testaments, between Judaism and Christianity. Christianity is rooted not only in the Old Testament, but also in apocalyptic literature. New Testament eschatology drew into its world-view the apocalyptic doctrine of the two ages. The expectation of an imminent end in the apocalyptics led directly to the watchful waiting of Jesus and Paul and John.

11. Is prophecy to be interpreted literally?

The Old Testament promised the coming of a Messiah, a descendant of Adam and Eve, a son of Abraham and David. He was to be born of a virgin, in Bethlehem, and would be called out of Egypt, but later out of Nazareth. He was to be righteous and holy, a lamb-like Man of peace, a Teacher, a Doer of mighty deeds. His ministry as a Servant was to find its climax in His death, a sacrifice for the sin of the world.

When Jesus was born into the world, all these prophecies, and many more, were written into history. Prophecy was literally fulfilled in the Christ-event. The New Testament writers, and the apostles in their preaching before the writing of the New Testament, found an abundance of literal correspondences between what was promised and what was fulfilled. These literal fulfillments included small details, such as His death on the cross without having any bones broken.

This literal fulfillment assures us that the Old Testament prophecies still unfulfilled, and the predictions of our Lord as recorded in the Gospels and of the apostles in the other books of the New Testament, will likewise become events in a real historic sense. We have good precedent for believing in the literal fulfillment of prophecy.

By "literal" we understand the plain meaning lying on the surface of language. David Cooper's rule is this: "When the plain sense of Scripture makes common sense, seek no other sense; therefore take every word at its primary, ordinary, usual, and literary meaning unless the facts of the context indicate clearly otherwise."

This literal sense is the customary, socially acknowledged meaning of the language used. It does not rule out the use of such literary devices as figures of speech. The Bible makes large use of imagery and verbal symbolism. The prophets were often poets, and poetry speaks in pictures. When Obadiah speaks of Jacob devouring Esau, we do not think of cannibalism.

Prophecy has a rich treasury of images which it would be absurd to interpret literally. Only a slavish literalism would say that, because Christ will come in the clouds, He could not come on a cloudless day. Such a literal interpretation can do great damage to truth. Biblical truth is often most effectually communicated in figurative analogies, like the lion-lamb which reappears in Revelation, or the army of locusts in Joel. Spiritual interpretation looks for spiritual meaning behind the literal meaning of words.

Language is not less certain and truthful because it is figurative. Normal interpretation is showing the divinely intended meaning, which may be given best through a figure. Literal need not mean material. We have a resurrection faith, but that is not, as some have sneered, a "dirt-slinging faith." To speak of the fire of hell, one is not required to tell what kind of fuel feeds that fire.

Let us admit that determining the right meaning of prophetic language is a chief problem of biblical interpretation. It is an important reason for differences among interpreters. Obscure passages must be understood in the light of clear and unmistakable truth. Our own resurrection does not seem unreasonable to one who believes that Jesus rose from the dead. Visions and symbols must be related to the basic affirmations of faith, and not used to set them aside. Since the New Testament clearly teaches that Christ was offered "once for all" (Hebrews 9:26), how could we argue from Ezekiel that animal sacrifices will in some future millennium be again prescribed for God's people?

12. What is the purpose of the Book of Revelation?

A father heard his son say again and again, "But you don't know how it ends." When the father asked what he meant, the boy explained that he was reading a book so interesting that he couldn't keep from turning to the last pages to see how it ended. Now he was telling the characters in the book, "But you don't know how it ends."

Revelation is the last book of the Bible. The whole Bible tells the story of redemption, and Revelation reveals how the story ends. It may not be wise to read every book that way, jumping from the middle complications to the solutions of the last chapter. But it's a good way to read the Bible. It's good to know that the story God has revealed to us has a happy ending.

The Book of Revelation fittingly closes the Bible with the word that God is not through with history. The Lord of history will bring history to its final and proper end. For God's people this will be a happy end. And so, like the Gospels and the Acts and the letters of the apostles, the message of this book is good news.

Chester K. Lehman has called Revelation a "tract for bad times." It was written in a day when the Christian church was suffering under Roman tyranny. Christians were ordered to affirm that Caesar is lord. They dared to say instead, "Jesus Christ is Lord," even at the price of martyrdom.

The Holy Spirit through John encouraged the church of his day by assuring it that God is acting in history, and that He will have the ultimate victory. In the conflict between the kingdom of Christ and the kingdom of Caesar, between God and Satan, Jesus is Victor.

The warnings and promises given to seven churches of Asia (chs. 2 and 3) have a timelessness which makes them apply to all believers to the end of this age.

The main body of the Book of Revelation (chs. 4-18) is like eighteen great panels in an art gallery. Each symbolic picture depicts Christ's work in relation to history. They are not incidents which happen one after the other; they may overlap each other. They portray God's triumph, on the earth, in history.

These panels give us some horrible pictures of sin and its awful effects. Evil characters appear: Satan, the dragon; the beast which is antichrist; the great harlot Babylon; the world system, falling in terrible judgment.

There is also the victorious Lamb, the Christ who triumphed in His death and resurrection. There is celestial joy, hallelujahs of victory for Christ's triumph.

The course of history comes to an end (chs. 19-22) in accordance with the purpose of the original creation. God completes His work. He creates a new order of things.

So Revelation concludes with the end of history, and a vision of the glory of the world to come. It is a happy ending, with evil eliminated and God triumphant. People from every nation will make up the people of God. Christ will be King of kings, and Lord of lords. In the world to come God will be all in all.

This is the way the story ends.

13. What is the "consummation"?

"Then cometh the end" (1 Corinthians 15:24).

What had a beginning in the creation, what has continued through the centuries and millennia, will also have an end. Some have called it "the end of the world." The theologians call it the "consummation." A Greek word for it is *telos*.

The consummation is the complete and final end toward which all things move. It is a finishing up of all that God has to do for us and say to us. It is the *omega,* the Greek zee (zed), the last word of prophecy. It completes and finishes God's plan for the ages.

It is the unfolding of the plot in all its meaning. A French word for this is *denouement* (de-noó-ma), which is often used to describe the last scene of a drama—here the divine plot.

The emphasis here is not only on Christ's second coming, but on what happens when He comes. The coming is the signal for a whole series of crisis events and developments.

It will be the end of evil. Satan will be headed for his binding, for the end of his slimy trail of deceit and lies. Evil men and evil causes will have gone as far as they can go. The antichrist, whoever he is, will be destroyed.

It will be a day of judgment, a time for God's wrath against sin. This has long been called doomsday. The accounting which men have ignored or defied, they will face.

The consummation will bring history to its goal.

The resurrection day will have come—the translation of living saints also.

The church, the bride of Christ, will be joyously joined to the Bridegroom. In a time of renewal the New Jerusalem will replace that which is outdated.

Salvation will have been completed, with all its effects turned into blessed experience.

The universal and totally effective messianic reign will have come. This will be the age of Jubilee blessing, which type and prophecy have foretold. Every knee shall bow to Christ, and perfect harmony with the will of God will become the order of the new age. Creation's imperfections will give way to a transformed world, delivered from the bondage of corruption into the glorious liberty of the children of God (Romans 8:21). The essential glory of Christ which was anticipated on the Mount of Transfiguration will be revealed in an outburst of heavenly magnificence, set forth in power and gleaming glory.

But all of this awaits His coming, when what has been

promised has been fulfilled, what has been begun comes to completion, when purpose becomes performance, when what we know in part we shall comprehend in its fullness. This is the consummation which Christ will bring at the end of our age, when He comes again.

14. How is eschatology related to evangelism?

The belief that Jesus Christ is coming again gives meaning to life, for it confirms the fact that we are going somewhere. Man was not created for one world but for two. This life takes on greater meaning when it is understood in the light of the other world. The other world overlaps this one. Mankind is made for the ages, and 50 million years from now I expect to be a young man living on with God. The relationship of eschatology to evangelism is that the return of Christ emphasizes the fact that life is more than what we share here and now, which motivates us to be prepared for the future.

However, in evangelism we should not use the doctrine of the second coming of Christ as a gimmick to manipulate people. We should not scare people with the doctrine of Christ's second coming, but rather teach this truth as a glorious anticipation that there is more to life than what we have here. The philosopher Emmanuel Kant said that man must be immortal, because he has too much potential to fulfill it in a mere seventy years. The truth of Christ's second coming is God's statement that He has an ultimate purpose for man that is not yet complete.

The second coming of Christ also emphasizes the larger dimensions of the kingdom of God. Jesus came preaching the kingdom of God (Matthew 4:17) and preaching the good news of the kingdom (Luke 4:43 and

8:1). This means that He announced the rule of God in a person's life. Wherever Jesus rules, there the kingdom is happening. Jesus said the kingdom is among us and we can get in on it. Further, He said the kingdom does not come by observation or organization, but is a spiritual phenomenon. Paul says in Romans 14:17, "For the kingdom of God is not eating and drinking, but righteousness and peace and joy in the Holy Spirit." This kingdom is being created by Jesus Christ. In 1 Corinthians 15 Paul says that Jesus will complete the building of His kingdom and then will turn it over to the Father. The second coming of Jesus Christ emphasizes the culmination, the completion of that kingdom. The details of the final phases of the kingdom in relation to the earthly scene are aspects which are discussed by eschatology. The one grand theme is that Jesus Christ is completing a kingdom, and that He will come again to culminate it.

The relation of eschatology to evangelism is the positive announcement that Jesus Christ is Victor at Calvary and will culminate His victory in the completion of His kingdom.

In evangelism the preaching of the second coming of Christ should always be done in the light of the climax of God's redemptive acts on man's behalf, the victory of Calvary and the resurrection. It is in the crucified God, risen from the dead, that we find deliverance from sin and release from the powers of darkness which have beset us.

Eschatology makes possible the affirmation in evangelistic preaching of our abiding hope in Christ, our assurance of His ultimate victory. It enables us to call people to identify with Him who is King of kings and

Lord of lords, and at whose name every knee shall bow.

We should, however, be careful that we do not simply play on the unusual themes that can be lifted out of apocalyptic literature, or simply use eschatological predictions as ways of manipulating people's interests rather than as honest treatments of the truth of the Scripture. Someone has said that you can classify missionaries in three categories: faith, hope, and love. There are those who go out simply teaching faith, that is, doctrinal concepts and proper confessional statements. Second, there are those who go out in missions or evangelism majoring on hope, talking most about the signs of the times, the nearness of Christ's return, and projections that this is the terminal generation. And, third, there are those whose mission and evangelism center in love, both as a ministry of compassion and as a word of God's reconciling love. It is the latter who have the more authentic ministry, helping persons come to know wholeness in their lives and meaningful relationships now, as they share the love of God in fellowship with Christ and with one another.

Many of the eschatological statements in the Bible are given in the context of God's loving concern that people be free from despair or any sense of futility as they anticipate the future. Paul is able to say in his treatment of the truth of the second coming, "Comfort one another with these words."

II

The Place of Christ in Prophecy

15. What is the chief focus of Old Testament prophecy?

"I will put enmity between thee and the woman, and between thy seed and her seed: he shall bruise thy head, and thou shalt bruise his heel" (Genesis 3:15).

These words addressed by God to the tempter serpent constitute what has been called the *protoevangelium,* or the gospel in a germ. It recognized the natural enmity between the snake and the man, and back of that, between Satan and God. Man, tempted by Satan, had sinned and lost his fellowship with God. Now God was promising through His Messiah Son, far down the centuries, to restore and redeem the lost human family.

Only the New Testament can describe this redemptive initiative of God. But the Old Testament foretells it. In the deliverance of Israel from Egypt and in the forms of the Old Testament worship the Old Testament pictures the redemption which God was purposing. And detail by detail Old Testament prophecy tells the story of a God who is coming to redeem.

The prophets proclaim "a God who comes." Salvation will be through visitation. Only as God comes to bring it can there be salvation and redemption. God will come in history, the prophets tell us, and bring history to its consummation. God will surely act redemptively in history, on the earth.

And so the Old Testament era is one of promise, waiting for that to happen which God has promised will happen. Old Testament prophecy has an open door to fulfillment. The plot calls not for more words, but for new deeds. And chiefly for a new actor: the Messiah, the Servant, the Savior, the Redeemer, the King, the Judge, the Lawgiver, the mighty Lord of all.

The Old Testament had its setting in the history and geography of the eastern Mediterranean world, in the time of the great empires: Egyptian, Hittite, Assyrian, Babylonian, Persian, Grecian, Roman. The prophets made many references to them, for their God was working in history. But the kingdom of God, of the coming Messiah, was their great concern.

This must be the great concern, too, of the student of prophecy. Some people years ago became quite excited about Nahum's lighted chariots that raged about the streets; they thought this was a prophecy of the automobile. And some today hear Ezekiel talking about communist Russia, and the Israeli nation of 1948. Was twentieth-century history the subject of Old Testament prophecy? Or was it the kingdom of Jesus the Messiah, the King who came and who comes and who will come?

This is not to deny that what is happening politically in our century has prophetic significance. It is interesting to watch how such developments as the worldwide growth of communism and the new emergence of a national Israel may fit into God's plans. But it was not on such details as national boundaries, and economic and social systems, and parliaments, and military strength that Old Testament prophecy was primarily focused.

The coming of God to judge and redeem and have and rule His people—this was the burden of the Old

Testament prophets. The coming in the incarnation, the pouring out of the Spirit, the growth of a new people of God—and then in the parousia, the resurrection of the dead, the judgment, and the kingdom of peace, this above all else is what New Testament prophecy is focused upon.

16. Why does prophecy center in the person and work of Jesus Christ?

"The testimony of Jesus is the spirit of prophecy" (Revelation 19:10).

"In the fulness of times, to sum up all things in Christ" (Ephesians 1:10).

Christ is the alpha and the omega, the first and the last, and everything in between.

The witness to Jesus is the sum and substance, the inspiring theme of all prophecy in both the Old and New Testaments. It all centers in who He is, what He says, and what He does.

In the life, death, and resurrection of Christ the kingdom of the prophets came to men. Christ is God in the flesh. God's utterances and acts in Christ sum up what God wants to do or say for us. On Calvary God and Satan fought the decisive battle between them. The battle continues, but already Christ is the Victor. The kingdom which came in grace and power through Jesus Christ will go on to its consummation in the new creation.

The Old Testament prophets spoke God's message on many topics: faithful obedience to God's commands, the requirements of basic morality and social justice, the certainty of judgment on every kind of unholy living. They made predictions about how God would deal with

His own people—Israel, and also the surrounding nations.

But above all they told of a coming day, when God's kingdom would be established. The changes to come would be wrought by a Person whom God would send to work His will among men. This Servant, who would be a Savior and Redeemer, would Himself be an atonement for sin. He would change men's hearts, and give them the power of the divine Spirit to live by the principles of the kingdom.

This coming One was Jesus. The prophecies about Him were written into the gospel. The testimony of Jesus became indeed the spirit of Old Testament prophecy.

And of New Testament prophecy too. The written Gospels tell the story of Jesus' coming and the substance of what He taught and what He did. The Acts and the epistles center on the church of Christ in His continuing ministry in the world. The Revelation shows the gospel of Christ in its consummation, with the purposes of God attained.

What else is there for prophecy to center in but Jesus? There is no key to prophetic truth but Him. He is the One who was to come, who came, who is coming. All of prophecy is comprehended in this.

17. Who is the Messiah?

A great figure rears His head over the Old Testament world—the Messiah. This name in Hebrew means chosen, or anointed. To begin with, he is David the king. But though David makes a great beginning as a king, a statesman, and a worship leader, the Old Testament prophets are looking for Someone greater.

He will come, they said, in the latter days, in the far-distant future. He will bring judgment and justice. He will reign in peace and righteousness. His eternal kingdom will restore the blessings and the fruitfulness of Eden.

The messianic era will feature not only material prosperity. The primary mission of the Messiah is in the spiritual realm. The Anointed One Himself will be uniquely righteous: holy, faithful, benevolent, merciful, just, compassionate. He will save His people from their sins and redeem them from all effects of sin.

From the time of the psalmists and the prophets the Jewish people looked for the Messiah and longed for the blessings His reign would bring. Every Jewish woman prayed that she might bring the Messiah to birth.

After the exile days political deliverance loomed large in the messianic hopes. As they suffered under Babylonian, Persian, Greek, and Roman domination, the Jews prayed for a deliverer who could give them national independence again.

This was the situation in New Testament times, when Jesus came. Judaism thought of the Messiah as coming in power and great glory. The apocalyptic writers had pictured Him as just such a One. The Pharisees all thought they knew how the messianic era would come. Their questions were only about who and when.

Jesus said He was the Messiah. In the synagogue at Nazareth He read one of the messianic passages from Isaiah, and claimed to be its fulfillment. He proved who He was, not by military generalship, but by His power over demons, disease, nature, and sin. He set spiritual and material things in the proper relation.

To the Pharisees Jesus was an utter disappointment.

Even His disciples, though they believed in Him, could not understand what kind of a Messiah He was. "We had hoped . . ." said the two on the way to Emmaus. How sad was the collapse of all their hopes after the crucifixion and before the resurrection.

Jesus told the discouraged John the Baptist that He was doing just what could be expected of the Messiah. Jesus the Savior was the Davidic Messiah and the Servant whom Isaiah had described. The work of the Messiah as given in the Psalms and the prophets pictures the heart of the gospel. So when the apostles preached the gospel of salvation through faith in Christ, they were proclaiming that the messianic era had come.

But not finally come. Christ must come a second time to complete the messianic mission. "Whoever says 'Messiah' says also 'eschatology,'" is the way one scholar says it. He means that only in developments at the end of our age will the ministry of the Messiah come to its fullness. It will take a second coming to give final demonstration that Jesus is indeed the Messiah.

Christ is the Greek word for Messiah. And so it is a word used throughout the New Testament as the name for Jesus. He is the Messiah, and in Him the messianic blessings have come, are coming, and will come. For the new heaven and the new earth will be the final stage of the messianic program.

18. Can we look for or accept any messiah other than Jesus?

Since Jesus came as the Christ, no other messiah can challenge or rival Him. No other messiah needs to come. No other has come, or should be expected. Jesus needs to come again to complete His work. We wait for Him, but not for some other messiah.

Jesus told us that others would come claiming to be the Christ, and would lead many astray (Matthew 24:5). This is being fulfilled in our day, and we need to be on our guard.

Sun Myung Moon, a Korean now living in the United States, is a well-known messianic claimant today. His movement is called the Unification Church. This persuasive leader has a host of followers, many of them young people. Moon has written the bible of the movement, called *Divine Principle.* It sets forth the doctrines of this so-called church, which Moon proclaims as a variation of Christianity, destined to supersede it.

Our chief concern is not the brainwashing and thought control of which the Unification Church is accused. It is the heretical theology which it teaches, including an eschatology. Moon presents himself as the "Lord of the Second Advent." As this lord he is a new person who can do what Jesus could not do. The crucifixion of Christ, he says, was a failure and a defeat for God's plans. Christians have been limited to a salvation which is only spiritual.

What God wants to accomplish, according to Moon, is the earthly salvation which is being wrought through the Lord of the second advent. An ideological war is being waged for world dominion. God's ideal is democracy. Atheistic communism is the Satanic contrast to God's earthly cause. The victory over communism, even now in process, will be achieved by AD 2000.

The Moon doctrine obviously rejects the Christ of the New Testament. It denies the cross and cross-bearing. It does not look for a future coming of Jesus as the Christ. It promises to substitute the program and the promises of the Unification Church. It calls for belief in a man rather than in the Son of God. It turns from the Son of righteousness, who arose like the sun, with healing in His wings, to a pallid and powerless "Moon." The testimony of Jesus remains the true spirit of prophecy. (See S. Mark Heim, *"Divine Principle* and the Second Advent," *Christian Century,* May 11, 1977.)

19. How is Old Testament prophecy related to New Testament prophecy?

Both Testaments of the Bible answer questions on prophecy. The Old Testament tells of a coming One, and promises the new age that He will bring. It opens the door to greater things. It points beyond itself.

What the Old Testament tells us is foundation truth. God had plans for the future. He had a purpose to redeem fallen man, and was going to send the Messiah to put that purpose into action. This Messiah would be both a Savior and a King. The ideas of salvation from sin and of a holy kingdom of the saved are rooted in the Old Testament. The Old gives them to the New.

But only when the Messiah came could the messianic idea be seen in its completeness. There had to be a Savior to bring salvation; there had to be a Redeemer to bring redemption. That Savior, that Redeemer was Jesus Christ. His person and work are set forth in the New Testament. The gospel which we believe and proclaim is the gospel of Christ.

The Old Testament is the Word of God, but not the final Word. It is incomplete, and finds its completeness in the New Testament. The Old Testament is an imperfect revelation only because God's perfect revelation in Jesus Christ needed to be seen and heard and preached and written. The Old Testament is a preparation for the gospel. It is a stage in the education of the people of God. But there was something more to follow. Promise had to find its fulfillment in Christ.

And so Old Testament prophecy was given in fragments and parts, one point here and another point there (Heb. 1:1, 2). We read it today in the light of its fulfillment in the events of history and in the first coming of Christ. We marvel at the truth of its concepts and the accuracy of its predictions. We are thankful for the larger book of prophecy which we have in the entire Bible, in both Testaments.

The center of New Testament prophecy is Christ, the chief Actor of the drama of redemption. His part is what was lacking. There had been many words—enough. The Old Testament prophets had spoken full and well. The apocalytists continued to speak after Malachi. But what they said was not accepted as adding to the revealed Scriptures. Everything was waiting for the new Person to come upon the stage.

Some teachers of prophecy today overemphasize the Old Testament. They talk about Christ being frustrated by Jewish rejection of the kingdom which He brought. And so, they say, He established a church instead. They think the present church age is a mere parenthesis between the reign He intended and the kingdom He will set up when He comes again. Primarily from the Old Testament they bring their notions of Jewish nationalism, a rebuilt temple, and restored animal sacrifices.

The two Testaments agree that redemption required the once-for-all death of Christ the Redeemer. The New Testament tells us that the Lord Christ already reigns over His kingdom. Spiritual applications become more and more important as the fullness of the purposes of grace is realized. We understand the Old Testament only as the meaning of the gospel of Christ becomes more and more clear to us.

The New Testament is the interpreter of the Old. The New Testament preachers and writers were inspired to give the meaning of the Old. They are the only inspired interpreters we have. The explanation of the Old Testament in the New Testament is a beginning point for all study of New Testament prophecy.

The New Testament looks forward too. The work of Christ was not finished when He was here the first time. There are Old Testament prophecies still to be fulfilled. And the apostles preached the New Testament gospel using Old Testament texts. Taking the two Testaments together gives us the overview from which the whole design becomes clearer. The Bible—the whole of it—has a unity and hangs together. But the key to its interpretation is the New Testament.

20. Does the New Testament look back to the first coming of Christ or forward to the second?

The answer is that it looks both ways.

Christianity is a historical faith. It is based on something that happened in history. What happened was that Jesus was born, lived, died, and rose from the dead. Those who knew Him believed Him to be the Christ. They were the first Christians. They preached Jesus as the divine Messiah. Those who accepted their message were organized into churches, which rapidly spread over the Mediterranean world. Today in every country live Christians who believe Christ died as their Savior and rose again as their Lord.

What Christians believe was soon written into the books of the New Testament. These books tell the story of Jesus and the early church. They look back to what happened: particularly to the death and resurrection of Christ. So the New Testament looks back to the very important history about Jesus and what the early church believed and taught about Him. First of all, then, the New Testament is history.

But second, the New Testament is prophecy, and looks to the second coming of Christ. It is concerned with the future as well as the past. Jesus told His disciples He was coming again, and from its beginning the church looked forward to that second coming. When the New Testament books were written, practically all of them included some prophecy about the future. In eleven of the twenty-seven books, every chapter says something about it. Every New Testament writer shares in predicting the second coming or what will occur then.

Now because the New Testament looks both backward and forward, one feels a certain tension as he reads. It is like when one wants to enter a busy highway. He stops and looks both ways. He needs to be conscious of both directions at the same time. There is a tension between the right and the left. Just so the reader of the New Testament must feel a healthy tension between the past and the future. He dare not disregard where we come from and where we are going. We look both ways: to the foundation and to the goal of our faith.

21. Why must Christ come again?

He came once. Was it the wrong time? Did He fail in doing what He was sent to do? Will He do something different when He comes again? What will He accomplish at His second coming?

The first coming was not a failure. Its accomplishments were tremendous. It revealed God in human form. Jesus taught God's truth. He set up the kingdom of heaven. By His death He accomplished redemption for sinful man. By His resurrection He canceled death's power. He established a church to proclaim the gospel of salvation.

But many of these things He only began to do. And these beginnings need to be completed. What He started needs to be carried on to its consummation. And that consummation will come at the time of the second coming. Then He will finish what He has begun.

Salvation needs to be finalized.

The redeemed need to be brought to spiritual maturity.

The kingdom needs to come to perfection.

His enemies—the antichrist and Satan—need to have the sentence against them carried out.

The power of His resurrection needs to be seen in the redemption of the created universe, and in the raising—or the changing—of human bodies.

Human sin and failure need to be brought to judgment.

The church needs to realize the triumph and glory which God has purposed.

The goals of history and of the created universe need to be achieved.

All of this got under way in Christ's first coming. That was not failure; it was tremendous accomplishment. But neither did it mark the ends of God's purposes. His plans which He wanted to bring to fulfillment in Christ His Son required the two comings: one at the climax, the turning point of sacred history; the other at the final unfolding of all things. We look back to what God has already done, which is tremendously important. But we know that was not enough, and that Christ must come again to write finis on the completed plans.

22. Is eschatology an essential part of Christian theology, or only supplementary to it?

Some people think eschatology is a hot potato, too hot to touch. They know about the differences people have, and think prophecy is just something to argue about. One young pastor said he does not preach on prophecy, for he has friends on both sides of the millennial question, and does not want to get in wrong with any of them.

Another reason Bible students don't study prophecy is that they don't get to it. Eschatology, since it is about "last things," is often the last chapter in the book of Bible doctrines. And the study group runs out of time before they get to prophecy.

And there are people who don't think it is important. We must study how to be saved, and how to live a Christian life, they say. But regarding what will happen in the future, we should just wait and see.

And so there are preachers who don't get around to preaching on the second coming of Christ. There are Christians who have never heard a sermon on the resurrection (even at a funeral), or on the judgment. In their theology eschatology is only an appendix, to be studied if you happen to be interested in it.

What are they losing?

They know only a part of the Christian faith. One third of the Bible is prophecy. It is sin to neglect or reject an integral part of the Bible. The whole content of the Christian faith is integrated toward the end. Without eschatology our understanding is incomplete about Christ, about salvation, about judgment, about the meaning of history, and the new age to which we are coming. Faith and hope are two aspects of one and the same thing.

Without prophecy we cannot fit our present time into God's plan of the ages: there is a present age and an age to come.

Without prophecy, we do not know the purposes of God. God has revealed much about the future; we should know what He said.

There is much mistaken teaching about the future. The best fortification against error is the clear teaching of Scripture.

Prophecy is the eye of Scripture; it gives us backsight, insight, and foresight. It tells us where we are going.

Eschatology, dealing with the things of the end, gives us the ultimate in meanings. What is the goal of history? What is eternal life? What rewards may we expect? Where do we go after death? What will we do in heaven or in hell? Without eschatology we cannot think through to eternal outcomes.

The precious promises of the Bible shine through as prophecies. How much comfort and joy we miss if we do not know them! "Comfort one another with these words" (1 Thessalonians 4:18).

Eschatology is a chief center of Christian doctrine, not a side trip. We need a recovery of prophetic comprehension, of genuine expectancy.

III

Promise and Assurance in Salvation History

23. What is the drama of redemption?

The main thread of Bible history is the story of God's redemption of fallen man. This story has been likened to a literary drama. The stage is this earth; the time, the centuries of human history. The drama begins in Genesis and ends in Revelation. It happens in real history, but has the features of a great creative masterpiece.

The drama has a cast of characters. God plays the lead role. He creates man for His glory, and saves him from his lost condition.

The enemy of God, the villain of the drama, is Satan, the devil. In an attempt to defeat the plan of God, he tempts man to sin and rebellion.

The rest of the characters are men and women in the service of either God or Satan.

The conflict between God and Satan follows a plot. Adam and Eve, the human race, fall before Satan's temptation, and God's good plan for them seems doomed to failure. But God announces a plan for redemption from that failure. He will send a Redeemer, Jesus, His Son, to accomplish this redemption by His death and by His resurrection.

The climax of the plot is the resurrection of Jesus from the dead. Those who believe in Him and accept Him can be saved from eternal death. The offer of that redemption is the good news of the gospel. The offer may be accepted or rejected. Each person must decide on life with Christ or death with Satan. We are now living in the period of this offer.

The drama comes to its denouement (unfolding) when Jesus comes again at the end of this period of choice to reign with His believers in an eternal kingdom. Those who have refused Him are condemned to endless death with Satan.

There is redemption from the effects of sin, but only for those who want it.

The drama has its important scenes of action. Yielding to Satan brings sin into the world with its consequences of death. The birth of Jesus was God's invasion of this lost world in the divine/human person of His Son. A Savior suffering on the cross brings life to those who will receive it. The power of Christ's resurrection gives to Satan the blow which will finally defeat him. The second coming of Christ is the consummation of God's plan.

At the end of the plot God triumphs over Satan and his purposes. Life overcomes death.

24. What is the high point of this drama?

The high point of any drama is the place in the plot upon which all the action turns. Sometimes this point is called the climax. It is not necessarily the place of highest interest. It is not the place where the problem comes to a solution; that is the denouement. It is where events take the turn which points to what that unfolding will be. The meaning of the action is what tells where the climax is.

Like in Shakespeare's *Othello*. In the third act, the general is finally convinced that he can no longer trust his wife. " 'Tis gone," he says as with a gesture he blows his love away. That is the climax of the plot; all that remains is to see how the tragedy will be worked out.

So in the divine drama of redemption. In the period of history before Christ the action was looking to the coming of the promised Redeemer. The appearance of a messianic Savior and King was foretold by the Mosaic forms of worship and by such prophetic passages as Isaiah 53.

Finally in the fullness of time (Galatians 4:4) the supreme Actor in this great drama was sent to play His parts as the incarnate God, the truth of God, as the sacrificial Lamb of God, and the triumphal Victor over Satan and sin and death. Probably the most climactic hour in this entire ministry was Christ's rising from the dead on Easter morning.

This was the climax of the drama. Everything before Christ looked forward to what He was to do in His incarnational ministry. After He returned to the Father, the message which was preached by the proclaimers of the gospel grew out of what He had said and done (Hebrews 9:28).

We are now living in the years which follow this climactic time of the first coming. We call it the gospel age. The preaching of the gospel proclaims the good news that the victory has been won. We look back as we proclaim what has already happened.

But we also look forward. The New Testament says Christ will come again. When He does, He will bring to triumphant completion what He began in His first coming. This is associated with what the New Testament calls "the end." This will be the denouement, the unfolding of the plot. The climax requires the denouement; the denouement is a logical, a theological, a practical fulfillment of the climax.

The crucial importance of the climax may be diagramed thus:

The beginning of the drama is the course of history from the creation of man to the incarnation (the ministry) of Christ. Christ, who calls Himself the alpha (the first letter of the Greek alphabet), first touched human history here, for He "was in the beginning with God. All things were made through him" (John 1:2, 3). We do not know how long this first section of the time line was; it lasted at least four thousand years.

The Incarnation

The Creation   The End

Changing the direction of the time line at the climax indicates the functional importance of what happens here. If the line were to continue straight ahead, the climax would merely be one point on the line.

But it is a turning point—the one fulcrum of all history. It is the end of the age of promise, and the beginning of the age of redemption, what we call the Gospel Age. Christ's coming brought something radically different. The good news of the gospel tells what that is.

The equal length in the diagram of the lines before and after the climax has no significance. We do not know how long the line will be between the climax and the end. Jesus also said He is the omega (the last letter of the Greek alphabet). The drama begins and ends with Him. Somewhere between the two was the climax.

25. How does what Christ has already done relate to what He will yet do?

Which is more important, Christ's first coming, or the second? Since they are both important, and get their meaning from each other, we dare not set one coming over against another as more important. We can look at which one came first, and understand why what He did then required something to follow it.

Some people make the second coming the great climax, as if the purpose of the first coming was only to prepare for the second. On the contrary, the New Testament makes it clear that what Christ did in His incarnational ministry—in His life and death and resurrection—was essential action in His plan of redemption. But it was not finished then, and it is His plan to bring beginnings to completion in a second coming.

We know who is coming, and we look forward with joy to His coming. For He was here before, and we have learned to know Him. It is His person as we have become acquainted with Him in the Gospels that has won our belief, our loyalty, and our love. His teachings and His promises have made us look forward to what He can yet do for us. If Christ were the one to whom something is being done in the prophetic future, then the end would have a very different character.

But He is the one who is doing it. He is the coming

One! We are not looking for *something to happen*. We are looking for *Someone to come* who already has been here, and who must come again to bring God's plan of redemption to its completion.

Eschatology is not only about last things, but about first things also. In Christ there is a unity of past, present, and future. What He will do when He comes again is not so much new things, as to bring beginnings to their purposed ends.

The resurrected life which we live in Him now will go on to the resurrection of our bodies. We are sons of the Father even now (2 Corinthians 6:18), but His coming will bring the day of our inheritance. The power of evil can be defeated even now by the power of the cross, (Colossians 2:14), but at the coming of Christ the prince of evil himself will be destroyed. Though we already experience Christ's healing powers, He must come to restore creation's lost harmony. Judgment of sin is in process already, but final judgment awaits the end.

It is not as though we were waiting for God to act. He has already acted, and will go on to finish His work. His first Advent brought saving grace; His second will perfect it. What Christ initiated in humiliation He will complete in glory. God acted dynamically in the person and the mission of Jesus two thousand years ago. At the end of the age He will reign in the full brightness of daylight. The day of consummation will be the sequence of the hope and promise of the gospel.

26. Is salvation past, present, or future?

"And in death save us." With words like these some Christians close their prayers. Others criticize this language. "That will be too late," they say. "You must be saved before you die, or you won't be saved at all."

To the question, "Are you saved?" some people reply, "I hope to be." That answer implies that only in the future may one be saved—that it would be presumtuous to claim that one is saved already.

Can one be saved now? If so, will he be saved at the end? Or do we get salvation only at the judgment or in the age to come?

The Bible has a great deal to say about salvation and being saved.

The Old Testament rejoices in "the Lord God of our salvation." Salvation is prominent in the messianic blessing promised by the psalmists (68:19) and the prophets (Habakkuk 3:18).

After the Messiah came, Paul wrote to Titus (2:11): "The grace of God that bringeth salvation hath appeared." Jesus, whose name means Savior, came to "save sinners" (1 Timothy 1:15). He told Zacchaeus, "Today is salvation come to this house" (Luke 19:9). The gospel, says Paul, "is the power of God unto salvation" (Romans 1:16).

To be saved was a present blessedness to many when Jesus was here. Salvation was no longer only a promise for the age to come. It was a gift for today. And so it was an experience to be entered into. Christians testified of the Christ "who saved us," as they said with joy. They had known what it was to grovel in guilt and sickness and ungodly living. Now at Jesus' word and by His power they experienced forgiveness and healing and victory over sin. They were saved!

And the salvation continued. It extended into the indefinite present. "He that endureth to the end shall be saved," said Jesus. This adds another tense to salvation.

Believers testify not only that they were saved at some point in the past. They continue to be saved. (See 1 Corinthians 1:18, RSV.) It is scriptural to say, "I am being saved." It is not presumption to accept day after day and year after year the salvation given us by a continuing Savior.

Then there is another salvation tense—the future. That comes through clearly in the New Testament. We live in the hope of salvation (1 Thessalonians 5:8). It is also scriptural to say, "I hoped to be saved." We are the heirs of salvation (Hebrews 1:14), but we will receive our inheritance in the future. Christ must come again "unto salvation" (Hebrews 9:28); that is, to bring salvation to completion and perfection. The end of our faith is salvation (1 Peter 1:9). Paul wrote that "now is salvation nearer to us than when we first believed" (Romans 13:11).

In Revelation 12 there is a vision of the end time, when Satan will be cast down. A great voice says, "Now is come the salvation" (v. 10). And in chapter 19 the great multitude in heaven shouts, "Salvation, and glory, and power, belong to our God" (v. 1).

The answer to our question, then, is, all three. Christ has saved us, He is saving us, and He will save us. The salvation which we have already is a taste and a promise of that which we will receive in finality when Christ comes again.

27. Is redemption past, present, or future?

Sin brings man into bondage. It makes him a slave. He is under the curse of condemnation. He is described in the Bible as lost, destined for eternal death. God created man to have communion with Him. But sin has broken that communion.

The slavery of Israel in Egypt is an Old Testament picture of defeat by spiritual enemies. But God rescued His chosen people from their bondage. They could not set themselves free. God delivered them from Egypt, and later from many other enemies. This is what He can do for sin-bound people today, and into eternity.

The Bible name for that deliverance is redemption; the verb form is redeem. Redeemer is one of the titles given to Jesus, who came to free us from our enemies, to bring us to blessing and well-being.

What is the date of our redemption? Our calendar tells us that it is almost two thousand years since Jesus came to bring us redemption. At that time He gave "his life as a ransom" (Mark 10:45). Eleven times in the New Testament is our redemption associated with the death or blood of Christ. His death on the cross was the ransom price. He became our redemption when He shed His precious blood (1 Peter 1:18). "We have our redemption through his blood" (Ephesians 1:7).

We already have it; we have been redeemed. We are the possession of a new Master, and sin no longer has dominion over us. We are even now a redeemed people, "a holy people, redeemed of the Lord" (Isaiah 62:12).

But redemption, like salvation, has its future tense. The Holy Spirit "is the first installment of our inheritance, so that we may finally come into full possession of redemption's prize" (Ephesians 1:14, Williams). Redemption was inaugurated by Christ's first coming; it will be finalized by the second. The day of full redemption is future (Ephesians 4:30). The signs of the end will say that "redemption draweth nigh" (Luke 21:28). The redemption of the body in the resurrection is the deliverance the creation longs for (Romans 8:23). Eternal redemption (Hebrews 9:12), like eternal life, had its beginning when Jesus was here with us. It will have its consummation when we are with Him in the eternal inheritance.

So redemption, like salvation, is past, present, and future. We have been redeemed, we are redeemed, we will be redeemed when Christ comes again.

28. When did Christ win His victory over Satan?

Many people are taking Satan seriously these days. Interest in demonism made a recent movie very popular. And devil-worship has grown into the cult of Satanism.

Bible-readers also must take Satan seriously. He appears as the villain early in the drama of salvation, and reappears constantly in the literature of redemption until he finally disappears forever in the lake of fire.

Satan and his host of evil have waged an agelong battle with God and His people. The contest began in the Garden of Eden, and Satan will be defeated, we are promised, in the consummation at the end of this age.

The story actually begins with a revolt in heaven, and continues with the unrelenting enmity of Satan against God and those who contend on His side for truth and right.

The major strategy against Satan has been God's sending His Son to defeat the evil powers by Christ's death on a Roman cross. Those persons who accept Christ as their Redeemer are rescued from the bondage of Satan, God's great enemy.

During Christ's ministry He once sent disciples out to announce and explain the arrival of His kingdom. When they came back they reported with joy that they had been able to cast out demons. Jesus' response to that was, "I beheld Satan fallen as lightning from heaven" (Luke 10:18). He did not say when it was that He saw this, but the context indicates that it had something to do with His mission here on earth. He had come to announce His rule. Satan could not resist Jesus, and fell from His place of power. The casting out of demons was a characteristic miracle of Jesus and the apostles. Satan already, it was evident, was on the way to defeat.

Another key passage to show Satan and his hosts in defeat during Christ's ministry is Colossians 2:15. When Christ died on the cross, Paul says, He won a victory over the evil powers. Satan was judged and condemned, and sentence was pronounced against him. It was now clear that the way of God was winning the battle. In this sense the death of Jesus is the time of victory.

We know from the New Testament, however, as well as from our observations, that Satan has continued his opposition. He is still seeking to rule this world, and does everything he can against the cause of Christ. Sentence has been pronounced against him, and he is doomed to final defeat. But the sentence has not yet been carried out. There is no doubt of the outcome. All the enemies of Jesus—Satan the chief of them—will be put under His feet (Hebrews 10:13).

That will be at the end of the age. The struggle of Satan will end at the close of history in a final triumph for our Lord. Christ's second coming will set the stage for the execution of Satan and his hosts. The accuser and deceiver will be cast down (Revelation 12:10), ultimately into the lake of fire (Revelation 20:10).

Even now the One who is in us is greater than he that

is in the world. Satan's power can be brought to nothing in our daily experience. And every present defeat of Satan makes his final defeat more certain. The destruction of evil, now and then, is one phase of human salvation.

So Christ has already won His victory over Satan. But the victory is not yet final. To finalize it is one reason why Christ must come again.

29. Why are Christians described as only heirs of the promise?

When a rich man like Howard Hughes dies, there is no lack of people who claim to be his heirs. Most of us at some time in our lives expect an inheritance.

The Bible makes large use of this idea of inheriting. We are the heirs of God, we are told (Romans 8:17). He has made us joint-heirs with His Son Jesus Christ, who is the "heir of all things" (Hebrews 1:2). In Him we shall inherit eternal life (Luke 10:25). In Him we inherit the kingdom (James 2:5). Since all things belong to God, and He has bequeathed it all to His Son, and in Christ all is given to us, we Christians are rich beyond description!

But just in promise? Are we wealthy only in prospect? Are we now poverty-stricken waifs, hoping that someday our ship of fortune will come in? Are we waiting in rags and hunger for what we only expect to have?

We have already received joy, peace, love, and grace. We have already received the Holy Spirit as a pledge, a down payment on the full inheritance (2 Corinthians 1:22; 5:5; Ephesians 1:14). Through the Spirit we already experience peace, power, joy, and guidance. We are richly provided with all that we need for life here and now. The foretaste of our inheritance is so satisfying and sufficient that we can only wonder what the full possession will be.

The down payment was promised, and the promise was fulfilled. It was promised that Christ would come, and He did come. Christ promised that He would send the Spirit; He did send Him, and continues to send Him into the hearts of those who believe and are willing to receive Him. Jesus died to ratify the covenant (Hebrews 9:15), and to make us certain that we shall receive the eternal inheritance promised to us. There is no question about the integrity of the One who has promised.

Heirs always look forward. Their interest is in what is coming to them. Their present is oriented toward their future.

The New Testament makes it clear that what we have here and now is only a partial payment of what God has promised. Full payment will come in the future, at the end of this age. Then we shall be no longer only heirs, but full possessors.

The first chapter of 1 Peter contrasts the sufferings of Christ, which were His when He was here before, and the glories that shall follow, when His true glory shall be revealed. He will come in power and great glory.

Likewise there is a contrast between the trials we may have now, when we are waiting as heirs, and the glories that we shall have then, when Christ delivers to us the full and glorious inheritance.

So we are only heirs now in this age. But then, after Christ has come again, we shall participate fully in what His estate has provided for us.

"He that overcometh shall inherit these things" (Revelation 21:7).

That's worth waiting for. And who would take a chance of missing it?

30. Was Pentecost a second coming of Christ?

John, in the fourteenth chapter of his gospel, reports what Jesus told His disciples in His farewell discourse. In verse 16 the three persons of the three-personed God are mentioned. Jesus, the Son, said He would ask the Father to send the Spirit to remain with the disciples. The Son, about to leave the earth, prayed His Father in heaven to send the Holy Spirit from heaven to be a Comforter to the disciples here on the earth.

In the same discourse (vv. 3, 18, 28) Jesus promised that though He was going away from His disciples, He would later return to them.

Ten days after Jesus' ascension to heaven, on the Day of Pentecost, the Holy Spirit fell upon the disciples as Jesus had promised. Was this also a fulfillment of Jesus' promise that He would come back? Jesus is God, and the Holy Spirit is God. Some people say that the coming of the Spirit, which after Pentecost has been repeated again and again as believers are baptized by the Holy Spirit, is also the second coming of Jesus. Therefore, they argue, we now look back to both comings of Jesus, the first and the second, instead of back to the first, and forward to the second.

Certainly Pentecost was a coming of God to man. It brought to the 120 in the upper room divine endowments of power, holiness, courage, abilities, and insights. It is evident that the coming of the Spirit inaugurated a new age of redemptive history. Paul spoke often of the life in Christ, or of His life in us. Christ lives in us and the Spirit lives in us—perhaps two descriptions of the same reality. Great are the spiritual blessings we have because God has come to us in this way.

Is this what Jesus meant when He said He would come again? No, there are good reasons to think He was telling us that He will come again at the end of the age—what most of us have always understood as the second coming of Christ.

All of the New Testament was written some years after Pentecost. And one of its important teachings is that the end will be a series of events which have not happened yet. Surely these cannot refer to Pentecost. The New Testament is oriented both toward the future and the past.

The gift of the Spirit is a pledge and anticipation of something greater still to come. The indwelling of the Spirit is an initial enjoyment of a life whose fullness is in the future. The Holy Spirit now groans within us in eager expectation of a glory that is to be revealed in God's own time.

The only mention in the Bible of a "second coming" is in Hebrews 9:28 ("shall appear a second time"). This is a prophecy, written long after Pentecost.

There is a clear relation between the coming of the Spirit and the second coming of Christ. The present reign of the Spirit in our lives, limited by our human imperfections, is a prophecy of perfection in the Spirit in the age to come.

The life in the Spirit is both a present experience and a hope for a still better future.

Yes, Pentecost was another coming of Christ: *a* coming but not *the* coming. It was a coming that is precious and indispensable to laboring and waiting believers. It was not the consummation.

Some prophecy study has been feverishly preoccupied with the future. So emphasis on Pentecost and the present life in the Spirit can give us helpful balance. But Pentecost must be seen as something realized in the mortal state, looking toward an ultimate spiritual state.

31. Is the Spirit-filled Christian now living in the age of the Spirit?

The answer is Yes and No. The question might better be put, In what sense are we already living in the age of the Holy Spirit, and in what sense are we not yet in the age of the Spirit?

The writer of the Gospel of John (7:39) said the Holy Spirit was not given until Jesus went back to heaven. To His disciples Jesus said that after He went away the Holy Spirit would come (John 16:7).

After this, on the Day of Pentecost, the Spirit did come. This marked the beginning of a new age. The Spirit has been and continues to be here in this age, indwelling all true Christians (Romans 8:9), bringing His gifts and bearing His fruit in their lives. There is a sense, certainly, in which this is the age of the Spirit.

Not all Christians are living in full surrender to the Spirit by which they received the new life in Christ. But insofar as they have been willing to allow Him, the Spirit has taken charge of their lives and has filled them with peace and power. They know by blessed experience that this is the new age of the Spirit which was promised.

But there is a sense in which the age of the Spirit has not yet come in the fullness of God's provision. Satan is still at work, and the world in which we live is full of evil. Multitudes follow Satan instead of the Spirit of God. Two kingdoms compete for loyalty, and evil is rampant. The new age of Spirit-enabled righteousness has come indeed, but the old age of unbelief and sin has not passed away.

This present evil age and the new age of the heavenly kingdom exist in the same historical scene, and in opposition to one another. Two ages have overlapped. The old age, which was here before Christ's kingdom began, is still here and will be until the judgment at the consummation. The new age began when Christ announced His kingdom, and when the Spirit came to begin the church. Because the Spirit is eternal and Christ's kingdom is eternal, the new age of the Spirit of course will not end with the second coming of Christ. The new age only comes into its full functioning then.

During this overlapping period people who are living in an evil environment and are subject to temptation may, if they choose, enter even now into the actual enjoyment of the blessings of the age to come. Those who receive the Spirit actually live already in this new age of the Spirit—an age which will continue eternally.

The end of the age of evil comes when Christ returns. The two ages will no longer overlap. In the resurrection these mortal bodies of ours will have been changed into immortal, spiritual bodies. The Spirit of God will have laid hold upon them, and they will serve His purposes alone. They will be immortal, with no physical weakness, and of course sinless. In that age, the ultimate age of the Spirit, He will be in complete control.

For instance, consider worship, the chief activity of heaven. Here our worship is hindered by limited understanding, physical weariness, and wandering minds. But there Christ will teach us how to worship. And the Spirit will not be hindered by our earthly weaknesses.

The age of the Spirit is here now. But its fullness awaits the end of this age and the coming of the next. "Maranatha."

32. Why is the second coming of Christ called a hope?

Do we say we *hope* Christ will come again simply because we are not *sure* He will? What is it to hope? Merely to wish? Like when we say we hope it will rain, not because there is a real prospect of rain, but only because our gardens need moisture. Or like when a girl stores things in a hope chest before she has any prospect of using them in a home and with a family of her own.

When we say we have a hope that Christ will appear in glory, the cynic may say, "That's all you *can* do, hope. Because you don't know, you can only do wishful hoping."

But usage has bled the basic meaning out of our English word "hope." The concept of hope is central in the New Testament. The word is used forty-eight times in the Acts and the epistles. And it is applied to things that Christians hold to be sure: the God of hope, Jesus Christ our hope, the hope of eternal life, of the gospel, of the resurrection, of salvation. Hope is a sure and steadfast anchor to the soul. It is laid up for us in heaven. It is a full assurance which we hold on to to the end. We rejoice in the hope of glory.

And so the biblical hope is a positive certainty, not a guess or a wish. It is an utterly unshakable assurance of that which shall be because God has promised.

Hope rests on God, not on man. It is God, not man, who has made the promises upon which our hope rests. And the character of God is behind the promise.

It is more than words. What God says He will do is consistent with what He has been doing. We hope for a program of action already in process. Jesus' first coming was the fulfillment of promise. He is the coming One, who said He will come again. We are waiting for the completion of something surely and gloriously begun. So surely, so gloriously, will it end.

In Titus 2:13 Paul assures us that our hope is a blessed one. It is blessed because in hope we were saved (Romans 8:24). We hope for a crown of righteousness (2 Timothy 4:8). In hope we await the grace which will be brought in the revelation of Christ at His coming (1 Peter 1:3).

What is it we hope for? The Greek in Titus 2:13 demands this translation: the appearing of the glory. "The Christian hope," says George Ladd, "is the visible appearing of the glory of God in Christ's return."

Our hope, writes G. T. Manley, has an immovable foundation, Jesus Christ (1 Timothy 1:4); a glorious Author, the God of hope (Romans 15:13); a wonderful object, eternal life (Titus 1:2); a precious effect, patience (1 Thessalonians 1:3); and an everlasting character (1 Corinthians 13:13).

The Book of 1 Peter is a message on Christian hope. It was written to a persecuted people. Persecution and hope belong together. God's tried people need a look that is up and beyond. They are on earth, but they have an inheritance that is in heaven. They are waiting for the Son from heaven (1 Thessalonians 1:10). They look for a city "whose builder and maker is God" (Hebrews 11:10).

A Scottish laborer said to Robert Louis Stevenson, "Him that has aye something ayont, need never be weary." The Christian hopes in One beyond who died, rose again, and ascended to the Father. He is coming again to receive us unto Himself. That certain coming is our hope.

33. How can we have assurance before the drama has come to its conclusion, or denouement?

In the drama of redemption (*cf.* questions 23 and 24) we now live between the climax, which took place in Christ's incarnational ministry, and the close of the age, when the curtain of the drama will be drawn.

We know and believe the climax part of this salvation history. How do we know that the end will become history too? What has happened we can believe. Can we also believe what has not yet happened?

Our main help here is to see the end as a part of a total action which, although it has not been completed, has already begun. The Word of God has said the Son, the Messiah, would come. He did come. It said He would die and rise again from the dead. That is what He did. It said the Holy Spirit would come. He did, at Pentecost. The forgiveness of sins and life in the Spirit have been and are joyful experiences to which multitudes can testify. It has happened and is happening. The Word of promise has become history.

The New Testament told what Christian living would be like between the times—between the beginning of the new age with Jesus' first coming, and the end of the old age at His second coming.

We were to pray for the coming of the kingdom (Matthew 6:10) and the coming of the Lord (Revelation 22:20). This we have done and will continue to do. But the prayers have not yet been answered.

A battle rages between Christ and the evil powers, and will to the end of the age (1 Corinthians 15:24). We share that battle both within and without, until Christ's return.

We participate in preaching the gospel to every nation, which is the program for us until the end (Mk. 13:10).

There is persecution and suffering for Christians. There have been more Christian martyrs in the past hundred years than in any previous century of history. We were told to expect this.

That is, we are following the program set up for us. The signs of the times are given for the period, not for a short time just before the end. The program will proceed to the programmed end. The *eschaton* has already begun. The elapsed time has been longer than many of us expected. But we were never told how long it would be—just that the end would come.

God has promised that the end will come, and He "is faithful who promised" (Hebrews 10:23). David Livingstone, that missionary-explorer who really put God to the test, phrased it this way: God is a Gentleman who never breaks His word.

The Maya language does not have a good word for "believe," and so the Maya Testament says, "Hang on to God." We have already experienced what God can and will do. Therefore, for all believers the denouement is as assured as the climax.

IV

The Church in God's Plan

34. When did the church have its beginning?

Basically, the New Testament church, the Christian church which will meet Christ when He comes again, had its beginning on the Day of Pentecost. But there is some background to keep in mind.

The 120 upon whom the Spirit came on Pentecost Day included the twelve disciples of Jesus and other Jewish believers. They knew that this was a turning point in history. They accepted the resurrection of Jesus as proof that He was the Savior-Redeemer whose coming was prophesied. Through Him was to come, in the last days, the kingdom blessings of the Messiah.

Now this experience of the baptism of the Holy Spirit was an introduction to the promised blessings of a new age. These people in the upper room saw themselves as a remnant of faith, as the true elect. The high point in the history of God's people had come. They were seeing God's redemptive program coming to a climax.

This was all in true sequence. God had been calling out since Abraham's time a people to receive His blessings and to accomplish His purposes. Then Jesus had come. He announced the kingdom and demonstrated it in His teachings and miraculous deeds. Most important, He had accomplished redemption by His death on the cross. By His resurrection He had asserted His lordship. He had now fulfilled His promise of the Spirit who should come to them. Of course they believed in Him!

This was a new order of things. Jesus had said He would build His church (Matthew 16:18). Now this building was under way. The power of the Spirit would empower all who believed in Jesus. It was their task and privilege to proclaim salvation through Jesus, and to bring into the church all those who accepted their message.

There was much to learn and much to do. They had to set the boundaries of this new fellowship. Should it be open to Gentiles? If it was, should they have to become Jews? They soon learned that race no longer counts, only a faith relationship. They saw that if God takes the Gentiles in, they cannot keep them out. And in Spirit-led conference among brethren they had to agree that faith in Christ and holy conduct must be the qualification for church membership, not such Jewish forms as circumcision and sacrifices.

As they gave up Jewish ritual and ethnic prejudice, they had to seek the Spirit's leading on such matters of conduct as worship of other gods and divorce and slavery. They had to develop Christian principles of stewardship.

They had to stress obedience to divine law and the guidance of the church, lest license overtake them.

To provide efficiency and order, they had to develop church organization and seek out leadership which would provide adequate administration and teaching and the means of evangelization.

Church history tells the story of these and many other developments. It began, however, with the coming of Christ and the Holy Spirit. Ours is the church age, framed between Pentecost and the return of Christ at the end of the age. The church will participate, of course, in the eternal kingdom and bring God eternal glory (Ephesians 3:21). But the church as we know it has earthly functions. It is enrolled in heaven (Hebrews 12:23), but lives and works here. It has something of an interim character. It is a bride, living in loving anticipation of the appearing of Christ, the Bridegroom.

35. How does the church relate to Old Testament Israel?

Paul calls the church (or churches) in Galatia the "Israel of God" (6:15). Is a New Testament church like Old Testament Israel? What are the similarities or the differences?

In both Testaments God chooses and creates a people. In Israel only a remnant is faithful. And unbelieving Jews, says Paul, are broken off. In the church only the faithful belong. The Old Testament Israel is ethnic, not necessarily spiritual. The New Testament Israel of God is the believing church.

Old Testament Israel and the church differ in that Israel only looked for Christ. The church knows Him, either in the flesh or by the tradition and the written Word. Israel never experienced the indwelling Spirit. The church lives in a light, a power, and a joy that Israel could not know.

The first coming of Jesus brought a new age. He announced the arrival of the kingdom. Messianic blessings began with Him. The coming of the Holy Spirit inaugurated the church age, with new spiritual reality. But the old age, which Israel knew, did not pass away. The new age and the old age coexist. In an evil setting the church is given power to display the truth and the love of the gospel. The old age will not close until Christ comes again.

Both Israel and the church were given a missionary responsibility to bring the nations to God. It is God's purpose to gather out of all nations a people for His name. Israel's missionary assignment came to a focus in Christ. Christ has laid the task upon the church.

Israel for many years was a nation (or two), with thrones, governments, sovereignty, territory, and armies. Even when they had lost their statehood to a series of invaders, they were ambitious to regain their independence. The hope, both of Jewish leaders and of Jesus' disciples, was that Jesus might become their political leader and restore their statehood again. But Jesus refused every effort to that end. The kingdom He brought was spiritual, not political. So the church does not have political goals.

Israel was a biological family, descendants of Abraham with common language, ethnic traits, customs, religious practices, and ancestral land. Even proselytes had to imitate ethnic Israelites so far as possible. The church broke down all racial and ethnic barriers, finding unity in Christ. Revelation gives us glimpses of the ultimate people of God, who come from every nation, tribe, people, and tongue (7:9). "All the nations shall come and worship before thee," we are told. (15:4).

Jewish Christians understood that the church was the new people of God, the people of a new covenant. They understood that the church stood in direct spiritual succession to the Old Testament faith and life. Cult forms were abolished, for their uses were fulfilled in Christ. Spiritual meanings of the Old Testament were continued in the faith and life and purposes of the church.

36. What things about Himself might Jesus have spoken on the road to Emmaus (Luke 24:27)?

The resurrected Jesus joined two believers as they took the seven-mile walk to their home on the afternoon of Easter Day. He talked to them about references to Him in the Old Testament Scriptures. What a privilege it would have been to hear that conversation! For one of our problems in the study of prophecy is to know which prophecies have been fulfilled in Jesus' first coming, and which we must still look forward to.

Later in Luke 24 we read that Jesus talked on these matters with others of His disciples before he ascended to heaven. This was good preparation for the Spirit-taught days ahead when they would have to use the Old Testament as a basis for their preaching, and as they were inspired to write the history, teachings, and prophecies of the New Testament.

Jesus used all three divisions of the Old Testament. First came the books of Moses, what we call the Pentateuch. The second part was the Prophets. The Former Prophets included the books from Joshua to Esther. The Latter Prophets extended from Isaiah to Malachi. The rest of the books in the Old Testament are the Writings, of which Psalms is by far the largest and most important.

A great many references in these sacred Scriptures concern Jesus, either directly or indirectly. It is not possible that the believers on the road to Emmaus that afternoon could have spoken about all of them. What are some that He might have picked out?

Quite likely He spoke about the Passover, from Exodus 12. He might have reminded them that as the Lamb of redemption, on an afternoon that very week,

He had died along with the last of legitimate Passover lambs.

He might have told them about His being lifted up on the cross as an antidote for the deadly poison of sin, just as the serpent which Moses made was raised up on a pole in the wilderness (Numbers 21; John 3).

From Isaiah, which is second only to Psalms in the number of references to Jesus, He could have referred to the servant songs (42, 49, 50, 53, and 61), the last of which He had read in the synagogue at Nazareth. He may have given the lead which Philip followed later in interpreting Isaiah 53 to the Ethiopian.

He may have introduced here the term New Testament (covenant) as He told them He had come to write the law upon their hearts. From Micah 4:2 he might have introduced the idea of a multinational church. From Zechariah 13:7 he may have suggested He was the Shepherd who had been smitten (Matthew 26:31).

Or He could have used all the time they had to draw attention to the messianic psalms (at least thirteen). He could have pointed out from Psalm 22 that "every sentence can be applied to Jesus without straining its meaning" (Sampey).

From Psalm 8 He could have shown that, having now come in humiliation, He must come again in full messianic glory. From Psalm 72 He could teach them that having been a Servant, He must come to make His sovereignty universal and eternal. In connection with the function of judgment for which He must come again, He could have shown that Ecclesiastes 12:14 teaches a final judgment.

No wonder their hearts burned within them as He opened to them the Scriptures!

37. How does the Great Commission fit into God's purpose?

A mural at the rear of a Greek church pictures the second coming of Christ. Thus the worshipers are admonished to return to daily tasks with the second coming always in view. They go forth carrying the gospel, to the end of the world and the end of the age.

"Gospel," in both the Greek and the English, means "good news." And news, especially good news, ought to be told. Jesus asked His followers in Matthew 28:19 to tell this news to every nation. And promising to be with us in this task throughout the days to the end of the age, He is informing us how long we are to share the gospel. What is the news we carry? (Reread the answers to questions 26 and 27).

So Jesus came to begin a new era. Through His death He redeemed fallen man and ushered in the age of salvation. He did not come to end anything. In the presence of the old age, salvation was offered. Salvation belongs to the age to come; it is an eschatological gift. But in Christ it can be received now. Announcing this is preaching the gospel.

The age of fulfillment is present, but the time of consummation awaits the age to come. The gospel offers us in present experience what the prophets had promised for the latter days. God wants everybody to receive this offer, to have this opportunity of salvation.

"All the nations" includes everybody. God's purpose was to gather a people, one united people, out of every tribe and tongue, obedient in faith and faithful in witness. The church was not to be national or geographic. Qualification for the fellowship of God's people was no longer to be social rank, education, wealth, or race.

Jesus broke with the idea of a chosen people, a favorite race. "Whosoever will" was His invitation; "saved by grace" is the slogan of the gospel age. This is what makes the gospel news. Such an open door was unprecedented.

In God's unfolding plan, the church was given the keys of the kingdom. At Pentecost the door was opened to the nations of the dispersion. In the house of Cornelius a Roman entered in. At Mars' Hill Greek philosophers could have become believers if they had not laughed off the opportunity. By AD 60 in Rome the Christian church was a Gentile fellowship, almost completely freed from Jewish associations. Stephen was the first to preach that temple worship and observance of the law were no longer necessary for Jewish Christians (Acts 7). If Israel refused to hear what Jesus taught, people of other races and languages and worship forms could replace them.

So the church is to be an expectant, evangelizing community. Proclaiming the gospel call is its chief responsibility. That Christ is coming again to receive His own and to judge the world is a part of the gospel. Because Christ is coming to the whole world, all the world must know about Him. The fruit of the gospel must be gathered from all nations.

The Great Commission sets the program for the people of God now. Evangelization will continue to the end of the age.

38. What is the significance of a world-encircling Christian church?

The preaching of the gospel and the building of the church began at Jerusalem, at the start of our age. From there, Jesus commanded, the gospel messengers should go through all Judea and Samaria to every part of the world.

Within the first generation, Christians preached the gospel as far away as Rome to the west, and probably India to the east. Through the centuries which followed, the gospel spread throughout the known world. Particularly during the past two centuries the church has branched out from Europe and North America into all parts of Asia, Africa, and South America.

Today Christianity is growing most rapidly in the newer lands. The era of missions has enabled people in almost every part of the world to hear the invitation to salvation, and to be instructed how to follow Jesus.

This accords with the Lord's program for this age. In fact, Jesus said that when the gospel has been preached in all the world (Matthew 24:14; cf. Mark 13:10), then the end would come. So this is an important sign of the end of the age.

Is our assigned task about accomplished? Has every nation heard the gospel? And so, is the second coming of Christ near at hand?

Some years ago we were told that the gospel had been preached in every country except Tibet and Outer Mongolia. But when has a nation heard? Surely before all the people are converted. There will be many unprepared when Christ comes. All Christians and churches still have much to do in evangelizing the new generations, and in teaching all things that Christ taught.

Christ could come now. There is nothing lacking, except more evangelizing. In mercy He tarries to give the church more time to evangelize, and the world more opportunity to accept and believe.

This fits in with the historic fact that there has been long delay, longer than the early church expected. We may be the last generation. But we need to work and plan within a perspective of still more delay.

There are some teachings of the New Testament that led the early church to expect Christ very soon (Mark 9:1). Some details of what Jesus prophesied did happen at the destruction of Jerusalem in AD 70. Passages like Matthew 24 and Mark 13 do not clearly distinguish between the near and the far future. The disciples knew that there was something to expect at the end of history. This, however, was inseparable from what God was now doing in the person and mission of Jesus. The same God, now acting to bring salvation, would act at the end of the age to bring redemption to its consummation.

In the sign of the new covenant Christians of every land have remembered Christ's atoning death in the hope and expectation of His coming again.

The Christian involvement in world mission shows an understanding that what God is now doing will find completion in the final deeds at the end. When will that time come? may be the wrong question. More important, how can the church make a faithful witness to the end?

39. Did the church of the first centuries expect Christ to return soon?

Peter asked Jesus about His plans for John's future. Jesus replied, "If I will that he tarry till I come, what is that to thee?" (John 21:21, 22). Peter probably thought of His coming within a man's natural lifetime. Yes, he was expecting Christ to come soon, and Jesus did not correct him.

The following quotations give us some clues on when New Testament writers expected Christ to return:

"Repent . . . that he may send the Christ who hath been appointed for you" (Acts 3:19-21). The sequence of thought in Peter's sermon in the temple is this: "You killed Jesus, but God raised Him from the dead; repent of your sins, so that God may forgive you and send Jesus back again as the prophets promised." Peter evidently thought the coming of Jesus would promptly follow the repentance.

"The time is shortened" (1 Corinthians 7:29). The obvious inference of the context is that Christ will probably come soon. Paul wanted the Corinthians to understand him thus.

"The Lord's coming is near" (James 5:8, NIV). Yes, the head of the church in Jerusalem must have had an early coming in mind.

"Set your hope fully upon the grace that is coming to you at the revelation of Jesus Christ" (1 Peter 1:13, RSV). Revelation is one of the words used for the second coming of Christ. The early church expected to see Christ in His glory soon.

"It is the last hour . . . even now have there arisen many antichrists; whereby we know that it is the last hour" (1 John 2:18). The signs of the end, such as the coming of the antichrist, are even now in process of being manifested, John wrote. The people whom he addressed thought the time was near.

So much for the expectation in the first century. Now for the second century. The epistle of Barnabas, one of the books in the New Testament Apocrypha, said this: "In six thousand years shall all things be consummated." The chronology of the Septuagint, the Greek

Old Testament at that time, placed the beginning of human history in 5500 BC. Christians of that time thought they were already well into the sixth millennium. The churches of the second century thought that the end of the age was near.

And the third century. Cyprian, one of the church fathers, wrote: "The day of pressure is even over our heads, and the consummation of all things approaches." Yes, in that century too they expected Christ to return soon.

These early churches were not mistaken or deceived. They just did not understand how God's time scale is bigger than ours. As Dean Alford, a great Bible scholar, once said, "God announces the events, and conceals for the most part in obscurity the 'times.' "

From them we should learn that we cannot date the end as either soon or far off.

40. What is chiliasm (millennialism)?

"Chiliasm" comes from a Greek word which means one thousand. "Millennialism" comes from a Latin word which means the same thing.

People who believe the doctrine of chiliasm are called chiliasts or millennialists (millenarians).

If you are a chiliast, you believe that after Christ's second coming He will reign on the earth for a thousand years. There are many variations in the details of this doctrine.

The biblical basis of the doctrine is Revelation 20:1-10. Six times in this passage the phrase "thousand years" appears. The chapter tells us that Satan will be bound at the beginning and loosed at the end for a little while. Martyred saints will reign with Christ. There will be two resurrections, we are told. We are not informed where these things will happen. Jerusalem is not mentioned, but Gog and Magog are.

At no other place in the Bible is there mention of these thousand years. Although there are no Old Testament quotations or clear allusions in this passage, some chiliasts think that a great body of Old Testament prophecy is to find its fulfillment at that time. No New Testament text says there will be at the end of this age a restored Jewish nation in Jerusalem. The Gospels and the epistles, in fact, say nothing about a millennial reign.

Chiliasm was believed and taught by a portion of the early church for several centuries. It fitted in with the expectation of Christ's early return. It was seen as a logical program for Christ and His church after His promised return in triumph. When Christ was here before, He did not reign as it was expected He would. This He would do when He came again, as the prophets had foretold.

This is the chief content of classic, historical chiliasm, which has appeared from time to time in the Christian era. The millennium is seen as a preparation for the ultimate kingdom of God. It corrects a merely personal hope. It argues that the kingdom must find an earthly as well as a heavenly perfection.

But chiliasm never received enough general acceptance to get this doctrine written into any of the ancient creeds, or into many modern ones.

41. What is postmillennialism?

One variety of belief about the thousand-year period is postmillennialism. This affirms that Christ will come to earth after the millennium is past.

Augustine (354-430) is said to be the father of postmillennialism. He rejected chiliasm, and taught that the church was the kingdom of God. He expected the growth of the church to overcome all evil before the return of the Lord. For him the thousand years were symbolical, meaning a long period.

Postmillennialism sees the rule of Christ in the church and the hearts of believers. The kingdom is extended or "built" by the preaching of the gospel. It is a long and slow process. Satan is bound as gospel influences spread throughout the world.

This view envisions the whole social order, including the state, brought under the lordship of Christ. It resulted in state and church becoming one, but the one was more like a state than a church. For fifteen hundred years this view prevailed. The Reformation got rid of some of the bad effects, but in most of Europe they kept the state church. Postmillennialists believe that the church is God's ultimate plan for human society on this earth.

This is the system of thought of liberal Christianity. Liberals throw aside any idea of Christ's coming again. They expect the era of peace, righteousness, and world betterment to come through the efforts of men.

But there is also an evangelical postmillennialism. Its followers have faith in the power of the gospel to transform society, and can cite for their encouragement changes in such areas as slavery and racism. They have seen the church make remarkable growth in non-Christian lands.

But two world wars and other chaotic conditions are hard on millennial hopes short of the coming of Christ, and this kind of millennialism is less common than sixty years ago.

Here is the postmillennial dream, in July 1776, of Timothy Dwight, president of Yale College and author of the hymn, "I Love Thy Kingdom, Lord":

"Here [in America] will be accomplished that remarkable Jewish tradition that the last 1000 years of the reign of time would, in imitation of the conclusion of the first week [of creation], become a glorious sabbath of peace, purity, and felicity. . . . This continent will be the principal seat of that new, that peculiar Kingdom, which shall be given to the saints of the Most High, that also was to be the last, the greatest, the happiest of all dominions."

42. What is amillennialism?

The meaning of amillennialism is indicated by another word with the same meaning—nonmillennialism. Amillennialists do not expect Christ to set up a political government on the earth. They are not millennialists at all in the usual sense of that word.

However, they do believe in the kingdom of God which is now functioning, and expect Christ at His coming to bring the fullness of the kingdom blessings. In that sense some see them as a kind of postmillennialists. Christ will come after the millennial reign they now know.

Most amillennialists are evangelicals and accept the Bible as the Word of God. But they spiritualize its teachings, and thus see the millennium as a spiritual kingdom and the first resurrection of Revelation 20 as the new birth.

They believe that many of the promises to Israel are fulfilled in Christ's relationship with the church. Therefore they do not see any special significance in present happenings in the country of Israel. Nor do they believe that Jewish birth is any guarantee of spiritual blessing.

Amillennialism does not expect any golden age here on earth. The ultimate blessing will be only in heaven. They see all phases of the consummation as belonging to the time of the second coming. They do not see a need for any period of time between the coming of Christ and the eternal state in heaven or hell.

According to the amillennialists, this age will end with the coming of Christ, a general resurrection of the dead, and a final judgment. The next age is the age to come of the Scriptures (Mark 10:30; Ephesians 1:21; 2:7). Amillenial eschatology is relatively simple and uncomplicated.

Most amillennialists have little to say about any future for the earth. The destruction by fire is complete and final in its effects. God has no further uses for the earth.

Amillennialism is probably the position of most people who have given little study to prophecy, as it is easier to understand. However, many good scholars also hold this view.

43. What is premillennialism?

When the Kellogg Peace Pact was signed in 1928, the American statesman for whom the pact was named, Frank B. Kellogg (1856-1937), said: "I am not so blind as to believe that the millennium has arrived." He was using the word "millennium" with the common meaning of utopia—some ideal state of society. Men have dreamed up many secular utopias. Any period of one thousand years is a millennium, but in common usage millennium means a period of great human happiness or human perfection.

The word came into our language from the reference in Revelation 20 to the reign of Christ upon the earth. As a proper noun the word refers to that time of universal peace and holiness.

Premillennialism is another variety of chiliasm. It is different from postmillennialism and amillennialism in its belief that the second coming of Christ will precede the new age of peace and holiness which millennialists expect. It takes different forms. All forms see it as a universal theocracy of a thousand years between the parousia, or second advent of Christ, and the eternal state.

Premillennialists expect a visible, personal advent of Christ to the earth at the end of the present age. Resurrected or translated saints of God will reign with Christ. Satan will no longer be free to tempt, harass, and deceive the subjects of Christ. Little help is given in Revelation 20 for knowing what this reign will be like. Will the seat of government be at Jerusalem? Who are the subjects? What will be the nature of the administration? Will it be a fulfillment of messianic prophecies? Will this be the throne of David? Will the Jewish people have some special place of privilege and authority? If it is in any sense a Jewish economy, will there be a temple and a revival of animal sacrifices?

Historical premillennialism is very reserved in its answers to such questions and scores of others which can be asked. It does not see Christian truth and principle as being in any way set aside. It sees the kingdom as having begun at the first Advent of Christ, and as entering another phase when Christ comes again. But it does not see the millennium as being the kingdom in full realization.

The millennium is only a step toward that perfection. The millennium is not the goal; just a step toward the goal. It is not the everlasting kingdom, but only an initial stage. It is not the house in which we shall live, but only the porch over which we shall walk.

It is important to see that one can be a premillennialist without crowding a lot of Old Testament promise into Revelation 20. We must let New Testament interpreters guide us into the proper placement of those promises. If we keep rein upon enthusiastic imaginations, anticipation of a millennium can be integrated in our theology and correct an interpretation that looks only for heaven.

Some great scholars have been pre's, among them Bengel, Alford, Lange, Fausset, Tregelles, and Lightfoot. At the present time the two leading positions in eschatology are amillennialism and premillennialism.

44. What is dispensationalism?

Frederick the Great, a Prussian ruler of the eighteenth century, once asked his chaplain for proof Christianity is true. "The Jews, your majesty," replied the chaplain.

Dispensationalism is a later form of premillennialism, only 130 years old. It maintains that in the millennium of Revelation 20 Christ will reign over a restored and converted Israel. At this time, say these interpreters, the Old Testament promises to Israel will be fulfilled in a material, political kingdom.

For this reason dispensationalists see great significance in the national revival of Israel in 1948. They are certain that God will give this nation of Israel victory over its enemies. This political development is a sign to them that Christ's coming is near.

Many Christians know little about the dispensationalist system. And yet they believe there is a connection between national Israel and the arrival of the millennium. That's probably what Frederick's chaplain had in mind.

Millennialism dates from the first Christian centuries. It reappeared as premillennialism after the Reformation.

But historical premillennialism is not the same as dispensationalism. All dispensationalists are premillennialists, but not all pre's are dispensationalists. Dispensationalism began in England after 1830. The chief person involved in developing it was J. N. Darby, a lawyer and a member of the Plymouth Brethren. His teaching was widely accepted in Europe and America.

Darby got the idea of a "rapture" of true believers from Margaret Macdonald, a Scotch woman who claimed it as a revelation. By rapture, a word which does not occur in the Bible, they meant a preliminary coming of Christ seven years before the real parousia (coming). The purpose of the rapture is to catch a selected group of believers away from the troubles of a seven-year "tribulation period." Thus the coming of Christ is in two stages: the *rapture,* a meeting in the air for the saints, and the *revelation,* in which Christ comes back *with* the saints to defeat an evil antichrist, and set up His millennial throne.

There are many differences now among dispensationalists. For instance, Darby expected a pre-tribulation "secret" rapture. Others have argued for a mid-tribulation or a post-tribulation rapture. For the Darbyites this was the complex time line:

A faithful minority in the midst of apostasy
A secret rapture, including the resurrection of Christ's
    own
A seven-year tribulation period—
    Withdrawal of the Holy Spirit
    A time of distress and martyrdom
    Conversion of "tribulation saints"
    Rule of the antichrist
    Jews serving as evangelists for Christ
    Battle of Armageddon in Palestine
    Rest of the Jews accepting Christ
Coming of Christ to reign with His saints in Jerusalem
The millennium—
    Satan bound
    Jewish sacrifices in a rebuilt temple
    Jewish dominance in the reign
    Peace of all nations under King Jesus
Satan loosed for a short time
    Massive rebellion
God's enemies defeated
Resurrection of the rest of the dead
Final judgment at Christ's throne
Eternal state—heaven and hell

In spite of its complexity, this scenario has been very popular for 150 years, 100 in America.

Dispensationalists insist that all premillennialists must logically adopt their systems. Since many have done so, dispensationalism is commonly assumed to be the same as premillennialism.

But increasingly careful and honest study has convinced many that they are historical pre's, not dispensationalists. They cannot accept the speculative interpretations of Darby or Scofield, who with his annotated Bible helped to popularize the system. For instance, consider these facts:

The same words in the New Testament are used for the "two" comings of Christ.

The New Testament says nothing about the return of Jews to Palestine.

Through Christ, the difference between Jew and Gentile is gone.

Christ's blood was shed on the cross once for all.

One can joyfully watch for the coming of Christ and believe in the rule of Christ upon the earth without being a dispensationalist.

45. What is transmillennialism?

Granted a millennium, what will this reign of Christ be like? Premillennialism makes it quite physical, an earthly political kingdom in which Jesus rules the world from a capitol in Jerusalem. Amillennialism rejects the idea of a future reign, or millennium, by seeing this reign as a present reality. Christ reigns spiritually in the church which He has liberated from the powers of darkness and given freedom to be the people of God.

Transmillennialism says with premillennialism that there is a future reign of Christ, an actual culmination, or telos, in which Christ completes His kingdom in a reign which demonstrates His ultimate victory. He then turns the kingdom over to the Father (1 Corinthians 15:24). With amillennialism this view emphasizes the present victory and reign of Christ among the redeemed.

Transmillennialism is not earthy, but is supra-earthly. This view sees the millennium as a literal reign of Christ. Literal may mean spiritual in nature, not material or earthy. For example, the resurrection of Jesus Christ was literal. He literally rose from the dead; however, His resurrected body was supranatural. (This is not the same as supernatural.) He had flesh and bones, for in His resurrection appearance Jesus said, "A spirit hath not flesh and bones as you behold me having" (Luke 24:39).

At the same time He was not bound by nor limited to the characteristics of the natural. He could come and go in a spiritual way even though the doors were closed. This literal resurrection, spiritual in nature, can be used as a key to interpret the meaning of the future dimensions of the reign of Christ, that which is called in Revelation 20 a thousand-year reign, which we have come to call the millennium.

Jesus' reign over the world is the final culmination of His victory for the created order. Though supranatural, it is not earthy and material. It is at the same time an ultimate spiritual victory and a literal happening. For example, the last part of Romans 8 refers to the creation waiting for a liberation. But this liberation is more than is often implied in saying that Jesus will "rule all the nations with a rod of iron" (Revelation 12:5) from Jerusalem. This liberation is consistent with the references to "a new heaven and a new earth wherein dwelleth righteousness" (2 Peter 3:13), which will supersede the present material order.

Further, to say that He will reign with His saints for a thousand years need not mean that His reign will be tied to this earth, using Christians to rule the different cities and provinces of the world's population. Rather, this reign may be something like a "spiritual internship in the heavens," in which we are introduced not only to a new age for this globe, but also to the vast resources which Jesus Christ has over principalities and powers and the total realms of the created order.

In this reign the enemies of Christ are defeated and

exposed. It is a triumph of the people of God. It will experience the presence of Christ among His people in a transcendent happening at the end of the age. Transmillennialism holds that this reign is supra-earthly and is the ultimate victory of Christ among His own and over the created order, as well as the exposure and defeat of the demonic which at the conclusion of this victory-reign of Christ are summoned by the demonic leader for the final encounter with God, which culminates in the ultimate final judgment.

Transmillennialism, with premillennialism, takes seriously the ultimate victory of Christ in a culmination which issues in the completion of His kingdom. This kingdom, while trans-earthly, is a literal fulfillment of the victory of Christ, unfolded in the scope of Scripture. He is the alpha and the omega, the beginning and the end. In all things He will have the preeminence (Colossians 1:18).

46. Is the church in God's eternal plan?

"Unto him be the glory in the church and in Christ Jesus unto all generations for ever and ever. Amen" (Ephesians 3:21).

With this benediction Paul closes one of the great discussions of the church. God will get eternal glory in the church. The Old Testament tells of God's purpose to have a people of His own made up of different nationalities. How He would do this was a mystery, says Paul. But the Old Testament prophets revealed much about this mystery.

However, it was only when Jesus came and the Spirit was sent that God revealed the mystery—how this people, the church, would be created in Christ. After it was begun in Israel, the church followed in direct continuity. The church found redemption through Christ. And after Pentecost the church proclaims redemption through the gospel to the end of the age.

The church in this age is only a foretaste and shadow of the perfection which will come beyond the parousia. Its members have imperfections and the church deals with human problems. It strives to do right but looks for ultimate perfection after the coming of Christ.

The church is an interim body, always with an eye on the future. It is now functioning in human situations. It evangelizes sinful men, and teaches them how to live holy lives. In heaven there will be no one to evangelize. The church baptizes new members and memorializes (only till He comes!) the first coming of Christ. It provides for administration that will probably not be needed in the world to come. It has to struggle with differences of understanding in our denominational situations. At the gates of heaven we will not ask to be shown where the Methodists or Baptists or Mennonites are!

Paul told the Ephesians that even now the powers of heaven are marveling at what grace has accomplished in us (Ephesians 3:10). Certainly we shall continue in the age to come to demonstrate the wisdom and love of God in saving us and bringing us to eternal joy.

The church is the goal-people of God. Of course we must be present when the goal is reached. We shall experience the redemption which God purposed from the foundation of the world. It will take all eternity for us to understand to the full what God did for us in Christ. Forever and ever we shall savor the experience of salvation and glory in the presence of our Lord.

Yes, the church is in God's eternal plan.

V
The Kingdom of Christ

47. What is the kingdom of Christ?

"The king of the Jews." This was the taunting jeer of the Roman executioners of Jesus. It was nailed to His cross above His head.

Was it all a cruel jest? When Pilate asked Him whether He was a king, Jesus replied, "Certainly I am." He was not the kind of a king the Romans knew. He was not the king the Jews were looking for, willing and able to mount the political throne of David. He was a preacher, a miracle-worker in behalf of the needy, and such a teacher as they had never heard before. But a king?

What kind of a king did the Old Testament prophets say was coming? He was to be the Messiah, the anointed servant, the Messenger of truth. He would bring in peace. He would establish eternal righteousness. His kingdom of holiness would endure forever. But the king Himself would be rejected and would die to save His subjects.

When Jesus came, He announced that a kingdom like this had arrived. He preached principles of truth and love. He called for repentance and for discipleship. His sovereignty was in the realm of the spirit.

The kingdom of God was the central message of Jesus. In Jesus that holy and divine kingdom came into history. He became the king not only of Israel, but of all people who would accept His rule.

Kurios Jesus—"Jesus is Lord"—became both the creed and the guiding principle of the early church. The kingdom of Christ became the rule of God, creating a people over whom Christ reigns. This kingdom does not have a geographic territory. It has instead a realm of action in which God's will is a living reality.

So the people who walked past Christ's cross could well be puzzled. Jesus had not looked nor acted like the kings of their experience. This was a new kind of kingdom, and Christ was a new kind of king. The kingdom of Christ is a way of believing and living and acting and serving. It is still that kind of a kingdom, and will be to the end of this age.

48. Is the kingdom of Christ past, present, or future?

Which one? All three.

It is past. The Old Testament writers, although they did not use the expression, kingdom of God, did often speak of God as a ruling King. "I am Jehovah, your Holy One, the Creator of Israel, your King" (Isaiah 43:15); "Thy kingdom is an everlasting kingdom" (Psalm 145:13).

These Old Testament writers also spoke of a future kingdom. "But they shall serve . . . David their king" (Jeremiah 30:9). "Jehovah will reign over them . . ." (Micah 4:7). Many details of this reign are pictured by the prophets. For centuries it was expected.

Then came John the Baptist, preaching in the wilderness, announcing that God was about to act. The kingdom would be introduced here on earth, in this age, by a messianic person (Matthew 3:2).

That person was Jesus. He said that the kingdom had arrived. The hope of the prophets was being fulfilled. Jesus told John that the fulfillment grew out of His person and ministry (Luke 7:21, 22). His kingly power and authority were at work. He made kingly claims all through His stay on earth.

Since Jesus came and taught and worked, since He died and rose again (Acts 5:31) the kingdom came, and it was indeed the kingdom of Christ. We look back on what happened then. And so, the kingdom of Christ is past.

It is present. Dispensationalists teach that Jesus came to bring the kingdom, in all its aspects. But since the Jews rejected Jesus, they refused His rule, and the kingdom was postponed to a later coming. And so this age is a parenthesis, they say, and there is no kingdom now at all. There can be no kingdom with an absent king.

The New Testament, however, says that the kingdom can be received here and now. Paul and others preached the kingdom of God (Acts 28:31). Believers were translated "into the kingdom of the Son of his love" (Colossians 1:13). And so, even today, we are in a present kingdom.

It is future. Many things that the prophets said about the kingdom have not yet been fulfilled; especially the judgment aspects. In the New Testament, teachings of a present kingdom are in the context of a future kingdom. The kingdom is even now in the world; it is also yet to come. The kingdom came with Christ's first coming. And it will come in all its fullness when He comes again.

The consummation of the kingdom has not yet occurred. Our bodies have not yet been redeemed, and we are subject to disease and death. Satan was defeated by Christ's death, but he is still in active rebellion against God. Evil persons are at work in a world festering with all kinds of evil. Creation is still groaning with imperfections. "We see not yet all things subjected to him" (Hebrews 2:8). The final victory is yet to come. And so the kingdom in its glory and eternal perfection awaits the great events at the end of history.

The kingdom of Christ is past, present, and future, all three. Hallelujah!

49. What is the difference between Christ's kingdom and a "Christian country" of our world?

The problem in the question is the meaning of "Christian country." Is it a country that has a state church, like England or Argentina? Is it a country in which there are many Christian churches? Is it a country in which most of the people are leading true Christian lives?

Since Christianity is a matter of Christian faith and discipleship, it hasn't much to do with nationality or race. True Christians belong to Christ's kingdom. There probably never has been a country in which all the people belonged to that kingdom. So there is no Christian country.

In Christ's kingdom, Christ is the sovereign Lord. Obedience and loyalty mark His followers. Among them there is an atmosphere of love and peace and kindly service.

A nation, whether it professes or not to be Christian, is ruled by a very human king (queen), president, premier, dictator, or other ruler.

Christ's kingdom is eternal: "He shall reign for ever and ever" (Revelation 11:15). That makes our question relevant to eschatology. Citizenship in Christ's kingdom has no terminus.

National governments come to an end—by military defeat, by elections, by coups, by economic failure, by judgment for moral failure.

In Christ's kingdom, the law by which the subjects live is the sovereign will of God. Right and wrong is determined by that will. A chief concern is to seek and find what God's will is.

In a nation, what is right is determined by arbitrary decree, constitution, and legislation. This human law may be related to divine law, or it may be contrary to it.

The kingdom of Christ is a part of the stream of redemptive history, with love as a motive, and salvation and mutual welfare as a goal.

In the kingdoms of this world there is a common grasping for power, wealth, and personal advantage. Personal selfishness is behind the social sins of violence, militarism, racism, economic greed, and cultural oppression.

The kingdom of Christ has a passionate, unchanging regard for human personality. Jesus gave an example for bringing good news to the poor, release to the captive, sight to the blind, liberty to those bound in sin, and wholeness to the sick.

In contrast, it is commonplace to find, even in "Christian" countries, injustice, caste, homelessness, hunger, and immorality of all kinds. People get their values and their models of conduct not from the Word and the people of God, but from the practice of the masses.

"The genius of Christ's kingdom is to ask in every problem situation, 'Who is the Lord?' " The people of the nations tend to ask, "What will be easiest for me and to my advantage?" These attitudes bring a difference in judgment at the end.

50. Wasn't the destruction of Jerusalem in AD 70 the end of an age?

In the year AD 70 the Roman armies completely destroyed the strongly fortified city of Jerusalem. After a short siege, Titus, the son of the emperor, captured the city, butchered thousands of the Jews, and left the temple area in such complete ruins, says Josephus, "that no one visiting the city would believe it had ever been inhabited."

Forty years before this happened, Jesus had foretold that not one stone of the beautiful temple would be left upon another. The fulfillment of this prophetic warning put a permanent stop to the Jewish effort to shake off the yoke of the Roman Empire. This did bring to an end all efforts of Jewish self-rule, until 1948. Since the temple was destroyed, all temple-centered worship came to an end, even to the present day.

The destruction of Jerusalem, then, is a sign of the passing of one age and the beginning of another. There is now a new covenant of faith, creating a true people of God replacing those who have refused the King and His rule. Tearfully, Jesus had warned of the fruits of rejection and disobedience (Matthew 21:43).

The destruction of Jerusalem is a judgment. But it is only the beginning of judgment. Its sad results are an indication of what is coming to all, Jew and Gentile, who refuse to accept Jesus as Lord, and to follow the call of the kingdom.

And so in the prophetic portions of the synoptic gospels Jesus speaks almost in the same breath of the judgment which is near, only forty years away, and the judgment which will be later, at the end of the age (Matthew 24; Mark 13; Luke 17). Jesus intermingled the historical events of history and the final event. The disciples had difficulty in keeping these two distinct. And so do we, in our interpretation of these apocalyptic passages. Certain details were fulfilled in AD 70. And other things will accompany the second coming of Christ.

The present age was introduced by the first coming of Christ, when He announced that the kingdom had arrived. But we are in a period of overlap. The new age has come and the old age is still here. Really, the destruction of Jerusalem did not end or start any age. It is simply an example and a symbol of divine judgment in this age. The judgments of history are rehearsals of the judgment to come. In this age the crises of history foreshadow the final crisis. AD 70 is a prelude to the ultimate showdown between the kingdom of God and the forces of evil and unbelief.

51. Will there be a seven-year "tribulation period" at the end of this age?

Tribulation? Yes. Jesus died on a cross, and His twelve disciples all suffered violence. Throughout the Christian era thousands of believers have been martyrs for their faith. Usually the persecutor was a state.

And some are suffering today—under non-Christian religions and forms of government which would like to stamp out Christian faith and practice.

This will continue to the end of the age. There is a spirit of antichrist in the world. Forces of unbelief oppose the truth and the right which Jesus brought to men. These forces will make a deadly final effort.

Jesus said there will be great tribulation just before His second coming (Matthew 24:21, 22, 29).

Christ did want us to know that the opposition to Him and His kingdom will grow more intense as the end approaches. But He did not leave us in any doubt about His final victory. "They overcame him because of the blood of the lamb" (Revelation 12:11).

A "tribulation period"? The New Testament does speak of "the tribulation—the great one" (Revelation 7:14). But such great trouble has visited the world from time to time and from place to place. The persecution of the early church by the Roman emperors no doubt seemed to the suffering ones like the great tribulation. The Anabaptists of Europe suffered terribly in the sixteenth century. The Book of Revelation, written in a time of persecution, tells God's people that they will be overcomers in "the hour of trial . . . which is to come upon the whole world" (Revelation 3:10).

In his vision John saw a great multitude, "out of every nation and of all tribes and peoples and tongues," which were saved "out of the great tribulation" (Revelation 7:9, 14). This sounds like the persecution of many times and places, not just of one "period."

Many dispensationalists have taught that the church will be spared the end-time tribulation by a preliminary "rapture" away from the earth and its troubles. Interpreting numbers from Daniel and Revelation, these people say that the "tribulation period" will be seven years long, and that much of the Book of Revelation is a description of it.

The uncertainty of the figuring they do is seen in their grouping into pre-, mid-, and post-tribulationists. These respective groups think that the rapture will occur at the beginning, in the middle, or at the end of the seven-year period.

We had better expect to experience tribulation, at some time, in some degree. We may see the more intense tribulation of the end times, and we may not. We must encourage one another in any trial, even if it be unto death.

Evil will last as long as our age lasts. It will finally and completely be defeated only in the age to come. The tribulation of the end times seems to be the birth pangs of the messianic age (Mark 13:8). Beyond suffering there will be glory.

It is not clear that we shall be kept out of tribulation. It is as sure as God's promise that we shall be kept in any tribulation we may go through. "Be thou faithful unto death, and I will give thee the crown of life" (Revelation 2:10).

52. *Is the present nation of Israel a fulfillment of prophecy?*

The New Testament says nothing about the formation of a Jewish state as a sign of the end of this age. And so, to say that present developments in Palestine are a fulfillment of prophecy goes beyond anything that our Lord or His apostles taught. Or at least, beyond anything written in the New Testament.

And yet, a great many people think that the state of Israel, established May 14, 1948, is a sign that Jesus is coming soon. The growth of Zionism and the migration of many Jews to Palestine fits into that. Where does this idea come from?

There are Old Testament promises of a return to this land by the descendants of Abraham. These were ad-

dressed to people scattered because of their unfaithful-
ness. They began to be fulfilled when Cyrus permitted
some of them to return to Jerusalem and rebuild a
temple about 500 BC.

The New Testament sees a larger fulfillment in the
blessings which came through Christ. James says in Acts
15:16-18 that the promise in Amos 9:11, 12 is fulfilled as
the Gentiles come into the Christian church. It is safe to
follow these inspired interpreters.

The dispensational system makes much of restoring
the Old Testament national and religious system. This
system requires that there be a large number of Jews in
Palestine during both the tribulation period and the
millennium which follows. And so for those who accept
that system, it seems that Jews going to Jerusalem are
doing it in fulfillment of prophecy. Some Christians are
certain that the state of Israel is a sure sign of an early
second coming, even if they are not dispensationalists.

The Old Testament promises to the Jews that they
would return to Jerusalem had an *if* in them. If you will
return to your God, then God will end your exile: this is
the sense of such passages as Deuteronomy 30:1-10 and
Jeremiah 29:10-14. God does not reward disobedience,
but obedience.

Israel has not as a people returned to God. Only a few
people are Christians in the state of Israel. It is not a
messianic state. Many of the people have no religion at
all.

God has not promised a mass national salvation to
the Jews or to any other nation. Salvation is for those
who believe in Christ. Jews have not been rejected, says
Paul in Romans 9-11. Salvation, not national independence, is Paul's subject. The way of salvation is

open to the remnant Jews who believe. Many Christians have faith that in the end times a great many Jews will turn to Christ. If so, they will be saved in the same way that Gentiles are saved. They will not be saved by their biological heritage, and they cannot be saved by migrating to Palestine. The privileges which once belonged to Israel have been transferred to those who believe. There is no biological or national spiritual privilege in this age.

53. Why has God preserved the Jewish people through the centuries?

He hasn't preserved them all. Great numbers of Israelites were destroyed by the Assyrians and again by the Babylonians when they were carried away into captivity. The ten tribes never came back as a whole (the "lost ten tribes"), although some individuals and families probably did. Anna, who welcomed the infant Jesus, was of the tribe of Asher (Luke 2:36). But the people as a whole became known as Jews, because of the predominance of the tribe of Judah.

After the Babylonian exile only some of the people came back to Jerusalem. The rest were scattered far and wide, as the "dispersion."

Another scattering followed the destruction of Jerusalem in AD 70. Thousands of Jews were slaughtered, and a long series of pogroms made the Jews a constantly threatened people. The most recent of these was Adolf Hitler's attempt to wipe out the Jews of Europe. Anti-Semitism is one of the ugliest facts of history. Professed Christians have been among the worst offenders.

But the pogroms did not annihilate the Jews; they are still here. Their preservation does look like a miracle.

We can't be sure just what God's purpose in this may be. And we wait to find out.

We do observe that it is only through Israel that God has made known His plans for the world. Almost all of the writers of the Bible were Jews. Three fourths of the Bible is Old Testament, and 95 percent of the Old Testament is about Israel. The Messiah was God incarnate in Jewish flesh. Israel is the instrument through whom God has revealed and carried out His saving purpose. He has not told us that He has no further use for that instrument.

God told Abraham that his children would bring blessings to the Gentile world. Israel was to be a witness to all nations. Their continued existence as an ethnic group is a testimony to the faithfulness of God.

Israel as a religious group continues in two lines: Judaism and the Christian church. Judaism is the continuing Old Testament community of faith. Because the church too has that line of descent, the church is more credible because Israel is still here.

The church continues to profit from its Jewish source. Its moral standards derive from the law of Moses as strengthened by Jesus. Its worship forms—the sacraments—developed from the Old Testament. The church's Holy Scriptures include the Old Testament. Its tradition of singing grew out of the psalms.

The picture in revelation of God's people for the future includes Jewish elements. It depicts Jews and Gentiles together in the peace and security and light of God's eternal purposes.

God still has something for the Jews to do in relation to King Jesus. Just how and when they will turn to Him is not yet revealed to us. The preservation of this people keeps them available for the divine plan—an instrument ready at hand for the Master Craftsman.

54. Are there valid reasons for believing in a future millennium?

There are many arguments about the millennium (cf. questions 40-45). Someone has said that though the millennium is to bring a reign of peace, the millennial question has caused almost two thousand years of theological war.

But the argument is not as serious as it may sound. George E. Ladd wrote that "American evangelicalism has placed an unwarranted emphasis on this doctrine" (*A Theology of the New Testament,* p. 204). None of the varieties of millennialism has been labeled an outright heresy. And no one view can claim to be the only Christian view.

Only extreme dispensationalism would deny that we are experiencing in the church age a reign of Christ in our hearts. So far as this earth and this period of history are concerned, His reign is partly veiled and His glory is under a cloud.

We all believe in the age to come (Ephesians 1:21), when God the Father will display supreme and fully revealed glory in the heavenly kingdom (1 Corinthians 15:24).

Is there a need for an intermediate reign here on earth, when God's will is done fully, in a history which is still counting years? Chiliasts feel that Christ's reign must be displayed publicly, with the veil removed. God's will in creation and redemption must reach its goal. Believers must share in the reign of Christ in this world.

There may well be an era in history when evil is

restrained and righteousness is triumphant. This will be the manifestation of Christ's glory on the earth.

Then there is the need for cosmic redemption. Paul said the creation is groaning for this (Romans 8:22). It would seem fitting for the same transitional period to provide for a moral, social, and spiritual utopia, and for a restoration of natural Edenic beauty and harmony.

Some people see a necessity for a restoration of Jewish political independence and power over the Gentile nations.

These are some of the reasons given for believing in an intermediate kingdom period between the present spiritual kingdom and the eternal reign in the age to come. But the New Testament nowhere explains the need for this tentative reign. At best it can only be a stage in the kingdom, an interregnum between two reigns, a porch to the eternal dwelling.

Such a period may in fact be ahead of us. But we cannot say it must be.

55. What will this millennium be like?

We must begin with Revelation 20, the only passage in the Bible that speaks of a thousand-year period, a millennium.

This passage mentions the thousand years six times. Unless this is a figure of speech, symbolic of a long time, we do have here a time measurement, a period of history before the timelessness of eternity.

Satan, who has headed the opposition to God throughout history, is made helpless by being bound. A chain is mentioned, which, since Satan is a spirit, must be a symbolic detail.

There are nations, such as Gog and Magog, at both

the beginning and the end of the period. A great number of people, like the sands of the sea from all over the world, are portrayed as being involved in the rebellion at the end. So the millennial reign does seem to be upon the earth.

However, there are thrones, and the thrones of the Revelation are generally in heaven.

Christ is the One who reigns, together with the souls of saints who have been martyred for the testimony of Jesus. These associates in the reign are spoken of as "priests of God and of Christ," which does not sound very political or military.

The millennium follows a first resurrection. A time of holy, utopian, messianic blessing, such as is described in the Old Testament prophets, is suggested.

However, we read nothing here of a restored Jewish nation in Jerusalem. There is no description of a regime of coercion, in which forces of irrepressible evil and incorrigible rebellion are held down by Christ's gestapo. It is a reign of Christ, and must be in agreement with the methods of grace and inner renewal which were introduced into the world by Jesus.

Whatever the millennium may be, very little is clearly revealed about it. Some millennialists can pile up descriptions.They do it by taking various messianic predictions in the Old Testament and arbitrarily finding their fulfillment in Revelation 20. That is reading meaning into the Bible rather than getting truth out by competent and careful study. We must guard against interpretations which are what we would like to think might be true.

At the end of the thousand years, Satan will be released for a little season from his bonds, and will lead the nations in a massive rebellion. Evidently this era of divine rule has not taken sin out of the hearts of the masses. They are very quickly deceived, and are lost in the end.

In Revelation 20 the rebellion is followed by two judgments. The first results in Satan's being cast into the lake of fire. The second is the judgment of the Great White Throne. All whose names are not found written in the book of life are also cast into the lake of fire.

If we do not know much about the millennium, we do know what its sequence of judgment is.

56. Is the millennium the eternal kingdom of God?

In Old Testament times the present was the era of the patriarchs, the prophets, the kings. It was the day of Abraham, Moses, David, Isaiah, and Ezra. The future was the day of promise, the new age of the Messiah, the coming One who would bring a better order of things, a golden age of righteousness.

When Jesus came, this new order arrived with Him. The promised kingdom was a part of the present. But included in the present was still the old order of sin and imperfection. It was a period of overlap. The old was still here. But the new order, the kingdom of God, was being experienced in the present of those who accepted it.

This is the period in which we now live. The present is full of blessing from Christ and the Spirit. And we have a future of promise, when the perfection of the kingdom will be fully realized.

The New Testament calls our present "this age," and our future "the age to come." This present age of history will close with Christ's second coming. The age to come will bring the eternal perfection of holiness and truth, when God's will is done in a new heaven and earth.

Some believe that Revelation 20 describes a final stage of our present, when Christ and His saints will reign on earth for a millennium of years.

Whatever form this reign may have, it must be clear that the millennium is not the eternal kingdom of God. A thousand years is a rather long time, but it is not an eternity. The millennium is simply a final period of history. It is a temporary house, not the eternal dwelling place (2 Corinthians 5:1). The millennium of Revelation 20 ends in a massive rebellion. Our Lord and His Christ shall reign, not for a thousand years, but forever and ever. However great may be the joy of a thousand-year reign, an eternal kingdom will bring still more joy (2 Peter 1:11).

The eternal God has made an eternal covenant (Romans 16:26; Hebrews 13:20). This eternity extends beyond any millennium.

57. Need we expect the rebuilding of a Jewish temple in Jerusalem?

The last Jewish temple, the one built by Herod the Great, was destroyed by the Roman legions in AD 70. Since that date there has been no Jewish temple in Jerusalem. And without a temple, there has been no central place for Jewish worship and the observance of the Mosaic ceremonies.

An important detail of dispensational thought is the Jewish character of the millennium. Jewish political control will center in Jerusalem, a temple will be rebuilt there, and Old Testament sacrifices will again be offered, say these interpreters.

From time to time there are reports of progress in plans to rebuild a temple on the spot where the temples of Solomon, Zerubbabel, and Herod stood. That would require, of course, the bulldozing of the Mosque of Omar, one of the most sacred shrines of the Islam religion.

The belief that a temple will be built there and that during the millennium animal sacrifices will again be offered there is based largely on the later chapters of the Old Testament prophecy of Ezekiel.

The New Testament prophesies the destruction of the temple (fulfilled in AD 70), but says nothing of a rebuilding. Hebrews, written to Jewish believers assures them that Jesus was the Mediator of a new covenant. The Mosaic covenant, represented in the temple and its sacrifices, was only "a copy and shadow of the heavenly things" (Hebrews 8:5). Christ was offered "once for all" (Hebrews 10:10), and so there is no more need for any sacrifice or any temple.

The revelator tells us that in the holy city there is no temple (Revelation 21:22).

Millennialists who talk about a rebuilt temple are driven to consider the sacrifices of Ezekiel's temple as only memorial in character. But a memorial is not needed, since Christ is present. The prophecy of Ezekiel's temple must find its fulfillment in Christ's dwelling in His people. In fact, the Book of Ezekiel closes with the phrase, "Jehovah is there."

58. Do the Scriptures teach cosmic redemption?

What will happen to our earth at the end of this age? Will it be destroyed and annihilated?

Second Peter, chapter three, speaks to this question.

Such words are used as dissolve, burn up, and melt. Most people have understood this passage to say that earth's end will come in a holocaust of fire.

Other prophecies speak of heaven and earth passing away, a phrase which seems to fit annihilation. Utter destruction suggests that the earth is hopelessly involved in the judgment of sinful man.

But the Greek word translated pass away means only to pass from one position in time or space to another. Peter speaks (2 Peter 3:6, 7) of two world judgments: one by water (the Flood), in which the world perished, but was not annihilated. The other will be by fire, in which the earth shall be burned up, but not necessarily annihilated.

Fire changes a substance into other forms: perhaps gases or ashes or heat. What is prophesied to happen may be a renovation of the earth to serve other purposes as a new earth. Jesus spoke (Matthew 19:28) of a regeneration, which usually means a change for the better. Peter prophesied the restoration of all things (Acts 3:21).

The clearest teaching on cosmic redemption is in Romans 8:18-23. Our redemption includes the resurrection of our bodies, Paul teaches. Redemption involves the spirit, but also the physical, the natural. To be complete, it must affect both spirit and body. The connection between physical humanity and the rest of nature is our bodies. Just as our bodies will be resurrected, so all of the creation is destined for liberation from the limitations under which it labors.

So we do not have a gloomy vision of cosmic failure, full of sorrow, grief, guilt, corruption, and death. The whole creation, Paul says, is waiting eagerly in neck-craning expectancy to step forth from the prison house and share in the glorious freedom of the sons of God. How much better is redemption than annihilation!

In the beginning God created the heavens and the earth and pronounced them good. But evil marred that creation. It suffers now under a curse of judgment.

However, earth cannot remain as it is, because Christ did not remain in His grave. God will create a new order of things for the completion of His work—in mankind and also in the lower orders of nature.

The answer to our question, then, is not quite as clearly affirmative as could be given to a question about the resurrection. The Scripture about the future of our earth is not as specific. It depends more on logic and analogy. And it is not spoken of as often.

Just how God plans to redeem the whole cosmos is not clear to us with our limited knowledge. But we can be assured that God's original purpose for His creation will be completely realized.

59. What is the "new earth"

Always God is making something new. Through Jeremiah (31:31) He promised a new covenant; through Isaiah (65:17), a new earth. A new testament came through Christ. Paul described a converted person as a new creature and a new man. The Christian's conversion through a new birth (John 3:3) hints at the final transformation of a sin-cursed earth at the end of the world. "We look for new heavens and a new earth, wherein dwelleth righteousness" (2 Peter 3:13).

A theology of creation runs through the Bible. To complete His work and accomplish His purposes, God creates a new order of things.

Men and women are creatures. The earth is the scene of their creaturely existence. The earth which is a paradise in Genesis is restored in Revelation to its original purity and beauty. The new earth which God promises will be the scene of the final goal of redemption.

God did not stop creating at the end of Creation Week. He has been making things new ever since, and promises that He will continue (Revelation 21:5) until He has created a new earth for the age to come. We see the final order of things unrolling under God's creative hand. The creation has suffered as a result of man's sin, but it will share also in the glory to be revealed.

The revelator combines in one vision the making of the new earth and the coming down of the holy city, the New Jerusalem, from God. It is neither a pale abstraction nor a heaven of sensual enjoyment. It will never be defiled by evil. It will be life filled to the brim with God's presence. It will be light and glory, holiness and peace.

The new earth, with the holy city as its center, is the final state of the eternal kingdom of God.

In *A Theology of the New Testament* (Eerdmans, 1974) George E. Ladd concludes with this paragraph:

"And so the Bible ends, with a redeemed society dwelling on a new earth that has been purged of all evil, with God dwelling in the midst of His people. This is the goal of the long course of redemptive history."

60. What is the goal of history?

"And then—and then—and then. . . ."

It is easy to write and to understand that kind of history. One thing happening after another. Mere chronological sequence. But—

"So then—so then—so then. . . ."

This kind of history is about things happening with direction. It tells why things happen. It is concerned with purposes and goals.

History has meaning only as the working out of the purposes of God. God had a reason for creating the world and putting people into it. That purpose is the production of the image of God in us for His glory. This is a goal which God has set, which gives a direction to history.

History records the attempts of the enemy, Satan, to defeat God's purpose. It also records the action of God for its accomplishment through Christ. Thus the content of all history is related to Jesus Christ.

There is a structure and an order in history which is divinely ordained. There is some flexibility, but God is always involved. He knows the beginning, the end, and the whole time line between. No human agency will succeed in obstructing His holy purpose.

God will not leave history to itself. He was in the stream of history in the incarnation of Christ, that He might accomplish redemption through Him. The process requires the things which will be done at the end of the age.

Prophecy is history become conscious—history expressing its meaning. In eschatology we have a philosophy of history.

Just as God was involved in the time-stream in the first coming of Christ, so He will enter it again in the second coming. History often seems to be chaos and confusion. But in the end Christ will bring order out of confusion and bring his story to its intended goal—a redeemed society in a redeemed universe.

Only God can fulfill the purpose of history. Man cannot do it, through the state or any other social structure. Social evolution leaves us disappointed. Social revolution leaves us frightened. The course of history must be seen as a whole in the perspective which eschatology gives us.

"What's the world coming to!" It is coming to the end God has intended. And it is the right end. The poet Byron spoke of the "deep melancholy of history." It often seems to be a tragedy. But Christ will turn this tragedy into comedy—a drama with a happy ending. The title of this victorious action is, "Christ in you, the hope of glory" (Colossians 1:27).

VI
The Coming
of Christ

61. What New Testament words are used for the second coming of Christ?

There is a vocabulary problem as we read in the New Testament about the second coming of Christ. How is that event referred to? It would have been convenient if there had been one Greek word which always meant "second coming," and which was always used by the writers to refer to that event.

But there was no word like that to use. Even the phrase "second coming" was never used, although once we are told that Christ "shall appear a second time" (Hebrews 9:28).

The writers, and no doubt the preachers, used a score of words and phrases to express this idea of the coming of Christ at the end of the age. Some called it "the day of Christ" (Philippians 1:10), "the day of God" (2 Peter 3:12), "that day" (2 Timothy 1:12), "the last day" (John 6:39), "the great day of his wrath" (Revelation 6:17). Others used "the end" (Matthew 24:6), "the end of the world" (Matthew 13:39), "the end of all things" (1 Peter 4:7). There were many other phrases like these.

Certain words which had other uses were also given this specialized meaning. The most common was "parousia." Its primary meaning is presence. The New Testament uses it to speak of the presence of Stephanos (1 Corinthians 16:17), of Titus (2 Corinthians 7:6), and of Paul (Philippians 1:26). Its usual translation is "coming."

Gradually this word came to mean Christ's final coming. Much more than any other, it is the New Testament word for this epochal coming, this momentous event. When used of Christ, parousia always refers to His final coming in glory. An example is 1 Thessalonians 2:19, "For what is our hope or joy, or crown of glorying? Are not even ye, before our Lord Jesus at his coming?"

Following the New Testament practice, theologians and Bible scholars use this word with this meaning. It would be good if its use would become common. It is a Bible word, as "second coming" is not. Its spelling has been taken over from the Greek equivalents, and it can be used as an English word, without underscoring or quotation marks. The pronunciation of parousia has been anglicized for English speakers (pa-rüź-ea), and no one need be afraid of its sounding too scholarly for a layman to use. Say the word aloud a few times, and you will feel at home with it. It is simply using a Greek word for the specialized meaning it has in the New Testament. And we have no other word to carry this meaning.

Another New Testament word with this meaning is *epiphaneia*. The English form is epiphany. It means a manifestation of the heavenly world to the eyes of men. It suggests Christ's appearing in glory surrounded by a host of angels. One instance of the use of this word is in Titus 2:13, "The blessed hope and appearing of the glory of the great God and our Saviour Jesus Christ." A word which we have for this—theophany—has in it the same stem that is in *epiphaneia*. An emphasis in the word is on the visibility of Christ's coming. Both words appear in 2 Thessalonians 2:8, "the *epiphaneia* of his *parousia*."

With this meaning of a visible appearance *epiphaneia* is used for both the first and the second comings (2 Timothy 1:10).

One other New Testament word is used for the parousia: apocalypse. The idea in this word is revelation, unveiling, disclosure. The Greek title of the Book of Revelation is Apocalypse of John. The word is translated "manifestation" in Romans 8:19 (AV), referring to the event of the parousia. The word is used also to describe the revelation of truth (Romans 16:25). But a number of times it refers to the end event, once (1 Corinthians 1:7, AV) being translated coming. That will be the time when the glory and the power that are His, now somewhat hidden, will be fully revealed to the world.

The future coming of Christ is an event of such a character that the Bible has used a varied vocabulary to bring out all of its aspects.

62. Isn't "rapture" another New Testament word for the parousia?

No. Rapture is an English word, derived from a Latin, not a Greek word. But the English word "rapture" is not found in any familiar English translation of the New Testament. And yet it is used more than any other in much of the writing and speaking of our day as the word for the parousia of Christ at the end of our age.

It has come into usage with this meaning through a phrase in 1 Thessalonians 4:17, where we are told that believers who are alive on the earth when Christ comes "shall . . . be caught up in the clouds to meet the Lord in the air." The Latin translation for "we shall be caught up" is *rapiemur*, from *rapere*. The past participle of this verb is *raptus*. From this our language has taken the noun "rapture," the verb "rapture," with its various forms, and even an adjective, "raptured."

Few abridged dictionaries will give an eschatological definition for this word. The reader will find only that rapture is "passionate feeling." It takes a dictionary like the *Third New International* to give as one meaning, "Christ's raising up of his true church and its members to a realm above the earth where the whole company will enjoy celestial bliss with its Lord."

As languages grow, it is common for a word to develop a specialized meaning which comes into common use. When there is need for a word, somebody is going to find or coin one that will serve the purpose. Rapture is such a word. It was used at first with quotes, showing that it was a new or unusual word. Sometimes it is still in quotes. But increasingly it is used and understood to relate to the way believers will meet Christ at His second coming.

Just as parousia became the common word in Greek, and also in English for Bible students, so rapture has been accepted by people in general.

The trouble is that rapture does not have the same meaning and emotional connotation for everybody. It came into use through the dispensationalists, who gave it their own specialized definition.

In the dispensational system there is to be a twofold coming of Christ. First there will be the rapture, called that because of the Latin word in 1 Thessalonians 4:17, which is the accepted description of the first phase of the coming of Christ. At that time the believers who have died are raised from the dead and go to be with Christ. The believers who are still living are the ones who are changed into a new celestial form. They are caught away also to be with Christ in a heavenly feast celebrating the marriage of Christ the Bridegroom and the church the bride.

It is taught by some dispensationalists that the rapture will be secret, unseen and unheard. Some imagine what it will be like when those not taken do not know what has happened to "the missing ones," those that were taken. Others speculate on the wild situations when Christian car-drivers or pilots are suddenly missing and their vehicles hurtle on with no one to control them. One writer has imagined what the newspapers will say the next day.

But the description in Thessalonians tells about a shout, the voice of an archangel, and the trump of God—hardly the marks of a secret rapture! "It's the noisiest chapter in the Bible" was one reader's reaction to the doctrine of a secret rapture.

In the dispensational sequence, the rapture is followed by a seven-year period of tribulation, in which most of the prophecies in Revelation are fulfilled. Out of an era of terrible persecution comes the rule of the antichrist, effective evangelism by converted Jews, and the gathering of nations for the Battle of Armageddon.

Next on this complicated program is the second phase of Christ's coming, called the revelation. He will defeat the antichrist and begin His millennial reign in Jerusalem. In this scheme there are two "second" comings.

But dispensationalists differ among themselves. Mid-tribulationists see this "third" coming 3 ½ years into the tribulation period. And post-tribulationists expect the coming at the end of the tribulation period.

An unknown proportion of Christians do not accept

this whole dispensational scheme. They can accept the above dictionary definition of rapture. But they are not happy to have their "blessed hope," the parousia of Christ, called a rapture, if it must carry with it all the dispensationalist baggage. They are glad to look forward to being caught away to be "forever with the Lord." But they do not like to call that event "the Great Snatch!"—as one best-seller does.

When people are told that the Bible is full of teaching on the rapture, and then cannot find the word even once in the translations they have, they can well be puzzled. Of course they may not find parousia either. But they can easily be told that it is a word from the Greek Bible, and that it means the coming of Christ.

63. What will the parousia be like?

Prophecy is one of the most important subjects of the Bible. Of prophecy, surely the most important event is the one which brings our age to an end. And so one would expect that the parousia would be described in great detail.

Wrong. Actually little is revealed about how Christ will come. This truth was not written to satisfy our curiosity. The greater attention is on who is coming. We wait for a Person, whose first coming to earth was the pivotal event of all history. He has promised that He will come again.

And so we are not looking for something to happen. We are waiting for Someone to come. The narrow and limited pathway of this life at some unexpected point will open up into the infinite, unimaginable prospects of the coming age. He will come to us, not we to Him, as we say we do in death. The initiative is His. The manner and the time are His. It is His sovereign act.

The word "parousia" was sometimes used for the arrival of a king or other offical person. "Behold, thy king cometh unto thee" (Zechariah 9:9) catches the idea, although this is not the primary meaning of that text. The Old Testament does not speak of the parousia in the New Testament sense.

There is a fitting suggestion in the word of majesty and honor, and of a formal reception. The Latin word which the church has used for centuries is "advent"— e.g., the first and second advents.

One should not try to image this too clearly. Nothing like it has ever happened, and our imaginings about it get rather wild. That is the trouble with the usual treatment by most plays and novels. These are supernatural concepts, difficult to put into words. None of us has any capability in celestial engineering. We had better just accept the facts, and leave the implementation to God.

We are given some details. However, we must recognize that figures of speech and the conventions of apocalyptic language may be used. It is helpful to know that Jesus will come on the clouds of heaven (Matthew 24:30), as He disappeared at the ascension (Acts 1:11). He will be visible, a sign in heaven. As the lightning is seen, so the coming will be seen (Matthew 24:27).

There will be the great sound of a trumpet as the angels are sent to gather the elect (Matthew 24:31). Accompanying this sound will be a mighty shout, an authoritative voice of the Lord or the archangel, or both (1 Thessalonians 4:16). It is futile and unnecessary to ask how even the brightest of appearances or the most ear-splitting sounds can get reception around the world. This isn't a job for radio or television. However God manages it, it will be something open and public.

As Christ comes, those who are prepared will go to meet Him (1 Thessalonians 4:17). "Caught up" suggests the sudden swoop of a swift, resistless, divine energy.

This tremendous hour will bring together all of God's own, both those who have died and those who are still living. We shall be caught up together. Even more heartwarming, we shall be united with the Lord, "and so shall we ever be with the Lord" (1 Thessalonians 4:17). In that tremendous event the realities of mortality and of time drop away.

In all this we may be sure of surprises. "I didn't know it would be like this!" But for the prepared it is not a fearsome prospect. It is the day for which we have longed. It is the dream fulfilled, the blessed hope realized. "Amen: come, Lord Jesus" (Revelation 22:20).

64. What developments will accompany the parousia?

What will Christ do next after His parousia? You may have seen charts which try to make clear a sequence of events in the program of the future. One Bible student's reaction to such a chart was that he was sure Christ wouldn't have to consult a chart to see what to do next!

For there is a program of transfer from this present world to the age to come. Christ, as the Lord of the ages, is the Administrator of this program. But more, He is the Program-Maker, and the program comes with its Maker.

The parousia is the key to the whole eschatological future. It opens the door to all the parts of this future. What are those parts or steps?

One is the resurrection. The loud call of the parousia

is a call that wakes the dead. The dead in Christ will hear that call and join the living saints at the meeting in the air.

Jesus taught, however, that "all that are in the tombs shall hear his voice," both those who have done good and those who have done evil (John 5:28, 29). The resurrection is an important part of the prophetic program.

Another part of that program is judgment—whether one or more. Judgment is a necessary step between the parousia and the eternal state.

One judgment is of the antichrist, or the man of sin (2 Thessalonians 2:3-8). It is the manifestation of the coming which will destroy this evil person. So that judgment may quickly follow the parousia.

Christ's appearing and His kingdom are mentioned together in 2 Timothy 4:1. The kingdom was introduced in Christ's first coming, and continues in the present period of the church. But the fullness of the kingdom must follow the parousia, either directly or over the millennial "porch." So the eternal kingdom awaits the parousia. In time, the parousia requires only the "twinkling of an eye" (1 Corinthians 15:52). It issues, however, into an endless eternity.

The present heaven and earth will continue until they are shaken by the parousia of Christ (Hebrew 12:27). They will be succeeded by the new heaven and the new earth of a redeemed natural order.

On this side of the parousia we await the revelation of Christ's glory. When the veil is removed, "we shall see him even as he is" (1 John 3:2). At the revelation of His glory we shall "rejoice with exceeding joy" (1 Peter 4:13). We await the glory of His presence, which is the parousia.

65. When will Christ come again?

Only God knows the answer to that question. When Jesus was here, He said to His disciples, "But of that day and hour knoweth no one, not even the angels of heaven, neither the Son, but the Father only" (Matthew 24:36). As a reason for always being ready, He said, "Ye know not the day nor the hour" (Matthew 25:13). Peter said, "The day of the Lord will come as a thief" (2 Peter 3:10), the kind of event that is never announced ahead.

Just before the ascension of Jesus, His disciples asked Him a question about the kingdom's time schedule. This was His reply: "It is not for you to know times or seasons" (Acts 1:7). You should not be asking such a question, He said. That is the father's business, not yours.

It is vulgar and irreverent to be stirring around in an area secret to God. God is sovereign in this. We know only what God has chosen to reveal—which on this subject is practically nothing.

Date-setting in prophecy study is foolish and wicked. Foolish, because the *when* of the end is known only to God. Wicked, because we are to live by faith, and should not be lusting for chronological knowledge. We ask *when.* He answers that we cannot be certain about the time, and so must always be watching and ready.

What we know is that God has planned the parousia, and that day by day the time is drawing nearer. We know that we must watch for the coming, always ready. What we do not know is just how He will come, and when. God has told us all we need to know. It is better not to search for what only God can know.

And yet preachers and teachers and writers of tracts, articles, and books continue to be preoccupied with setting dates for the coming. They have been doing this for centuries. Usually now they do it approximately by saying it must be in this generation or this century.

Of all this stuff, what shall I read? As soon as the author begins to set dates, I quit reading. When the preacher claims to know what Jesus said no man can know, I quit listening.

I have even stopped saying that Jesus is coming soon, although with some people a belief in the "soon coming" is a mark of orthodoxy. If when I say that the coming will be soon I mean that it is imminent, that it may be today, then I can say that. But most people do not understand the phrase that way. They think it means this week, or this month, or this decade, or at least this century. That is what I thought it meant when I heard it seventy-five years ago.

Now remember, Christ may come that soon. But it is more than we know that He will. We should not give as truth what we do not know is true.

Augustine said it this way many centuries ago: "He who loves the coming of the Lord is not he who affirms it is far off, nor is it he who says it is near. It is he who, whether it be far or near, awaits it with sincere faith, steadfast hope, and fervent love."

66. Don't recent signs indicate that the parousia is near?

Yes, there are many "signs of the times" that make it easy to believe that the "end of the world" is near. Jesus gave some of them, and Paul and John gave others.

One of the leading ones is the preaching of the gospel in all the world (Matthew 24:14). Whether through the teaching of missionaries, or the translation of the Bible into languages of the world's people, or the use of air-waves in radio and television, the gospel is even now known worldwide. Jesus did not say that everybody would believe and be saved. He did tell us many would be unprepared to meet Him when He came. So there is nothing about this sign that would make the parousia impossible today.

Another sign is the great tribulation and persecution associated with the end of this age. Matthew 24 is one of the passages to read on this. However, one must remember that this Scripture describes two great tragedies of judgment.

The first is the destruction of Jerusalem by the Romans in AD 70, thirty years after Jesus spoke the Olivet Discourse. This was an awful horror in which a million Jews were cruelly starved and slaughtered, and their center of worship was completely destroyed, and has never been rebuilt.

The second tragedy of this chapter is another time of awful persecution and devastation, sometimes called the "tribulation period." The divine judgment of past history has been a rehearsal of a similar judgment to come.

Has this judgment of the endtime come yet? History is full of tragic horror, like the persecutions of Christians by the Roman emperors, by papal inquisitors, by the state churches of Reformation times, by rightist and leftist governments. We just can't say whether the ultimate showdown between God and the demonic is as yet preparing the way for the end.

Other signs are world-shaking political events and convulsions of nature. Such conditions have always been present—wars, crime waves, and famines. They might be coming in greater concentration as the age draws toward the end, but it is hard to prove that.

The appearance of the antichrist—the man of sin—should be a sure sign. For he is to be destroyed by the manifestation of Christ (2 Thessalonians 2:8). But since the antichrist might be a system of thought, like atheism, or a government, like communism, it is hard to say when he has arrived.

Signs of Christ's coming can be helpful in showing that God moves in an orderly way toward the goal of history. But simply as a way of telling how far from the end we are, we don't need signs. If we live in faith and readiness, we don't ask how near or how far. Jesus said it is an evil generation which asks for signs. We can leave all matters of time with the Lord of history.

67. Is it only recently that the "soon coming" has been expected?

In the first centuries of this era Christians were expecting the early consummation of the age. (See question 39.) This continued also after Augustine (AD 430).

Gregory the Great, who became pope in 590, thought the end was near because of "the most unspeakable Lombards."

Joachim of Fiore, an apocalyptic monk, arguing that a day is a year (Revelation 11:3), thought the end would come in 1260, when Frederick II planned a crusade for the capture of Jerusalem. But the excitement cooled down when this emperor died in 1250.

Luther in 1530 made the German translation of Daniel ahead of its turn so people could read it before the terrible "day of the Lord."

Bernard Rothman, an Anabaptist, figured ingeniously from numbers in the Bible that the Reformation would bring Christ to Germany in 1533.

John Napier (1550-1617), the Scottish inventor of logarithms, used his tables to compute the date of the coming—between 1688 and 1700. His commentary on Revelation went through twenty-three editions before 1700. After that, of course, it was not so popular. Sir Thomas Browne, an English writer of the seventeenth century, said: "That general opinion that the world grows near its end, hath possessed all ages as nearly as our own."

A History of the Plymouth Brethren (Neatby, 1901) says, "If anyone had told the first Brethren that three quarters of a century might elapse and the church be still on earth, the answer would probably have been a smile, partly of pity, partly of disapproval, wholly of incredulity." The "soon and secret" coming has now been expected by the dispensationalists for a century and a half.

William Miller, an Adventist, set 1843, and later 1844, as the great day.

Jehovah's Witnesses first announced 1874 as the end of the present world system. They later made it 1914, 1915, and 1975. A new date will probably be set soon!

Shortly after the turn of this century Mennonites of America began to listen to preaching which assured them that the coming was within sight. In August 1903, I heard one of these prophets tell a congregation of Kansas farmers that it would be useless for them to sow wheat that fall, for the Lord would return before they could harvest the crop. Years afterward this man said his mistake was in "localizing" prophecy.

The most tragic disappointment of the Mennonites with such date-setting was in Russia about one hundred years ago. A large number of these nonviolent peace-lovers were finding new homes and religious freedom in North America. A smaller group went the opposite direction in flight from a military antichrist. They were influenced by a German pietist, Heinrich Jung-Stilling. This author's novel *Homesickness* led some Mennonites to accept a withdrawal millennialism. Claas Epp, Jr., built up a following which was persuaded to look to the East to Turkestan, east of the Caspian Sea, where they expected Christ to come and, according to the biblical interpretations of Epp, to set up a spiritual-economic-political reign.

Epp's eschatology became increasingly radical. He asserted that Christ would come to this Turkestan remnant of His people soon, within a decade. Finally he announced March 8, 1889, as the great day. He took a "throne" on a table in the churchyard. All day the congregation, dressed in white robes, fasted and prayed. Epp told the group the Lord had tarried. Three times that day they returned and watched in vain.

Two years later Epp announced a postponed second coming. He made other irrational claims, and many left his community. Epp died of cancer in 1913. The complex tragedy of his life and the Great Trek to an Eastern wilderness was due largely to a controversial and fanatical eschatology. It is a chapter of Mennonite history which should not be forgotten, for it has much to teach about what a biblical and spiritual eschatology should be.

But many thousands of people are buying the books and listening to the preaching of others who may lead them into a wilderness quite as disappointing as Epp's trek into the Russian East. Hal Lindsay's *The Terminal*

Generation and other earlier books set dates for the end. In a recent newspaper interview he says, "It's now a definite countdown. I would suspect that all of this would be brought to fulfillment before the year 2000."

One of the recent episodes to get attention is the vigil the Nance clan carried on for months in 1975-76 at Grannis, Arkansas. An aunt, Viola Walker, had received a message from God that the coming of Christ was at hand.

It is important to know that people have been saying things like that for almost 2000 years. And they have been mistaken. What they have said brings the whole study of eschatology into disrepute. It deprives people of truth they ought to have as they turn from the calendar-makers in disgust.

As H. Thielicke has noted, "This brooding over the position of the hands on the clock of the world is something that does not concern you. God alone knows when the midnight hour will come. Speculation about this question only leads you away from the real task which is assigned to you."

68. Why are questions of the time and the manner of the parousia of little importance?

Questions about the *when* and the *how* are of little importance because questions about the *who* and the *what* and the *why* receive more attention in the Scriptures.

About the One *who* is coming we hear again and again. There's no doubt about this at all. Jesus who came once is coming again. Of that there's no doubt or question or argument.

And on the *what* we have a score of words and phrases. (See question 63.) We don't need to visualize or imagine just how it's going to take place, if we know what it is that is promised: a presence, a power, a glory, a manifestation, a theophany, an unveiling, a consummation. The Scriptures tell us a great deal about what it is that we are hoping for.

And the Bible tells us much about *why* Christ is coming: to complete our redemption of His work of salvation, to perfect His kingdom, to defeat His enemies, to raise the dead, to sit in final judgment, to perfect His purposes and achieve His goals. This is what eschatology is all about, and the Bible has many chapters and books to describe and discuss it.

In contrast, Jesus and the writers of the New Testament tell us very little about just when Jesus is coming, and what that coming will be like. Enough to prepare us for the event, but not enough to satisfy the kind of curiosity that most people seem to have. And so writers bid for bigger sales and speakers try to attract larger crowds by stimulating curiosity and raising questions that no one knows enough to answer. Therefore the subject lends itself to a sensationalism that is out of place in the search for religious truth and the walk of Christian faith.

There is a sober and modest study about the future in its relation to the past and the present. It is called eschatology; a more common word is prophecy. It is a respectable, important, and essential part of biblical theology.

But so much "prophecy" teaching is given to speculation and clashes of opinion between the schools of interpretation that many Christian people think it is only for radicals and cranks. They would be hungry for the *who* and the *what* and the *why* of eschatology, but they are repelled by the *when* and the *how*.

The Christian hope of Christ's parousia has the power to unite God's people as they watch together for the fulfillment of God's promises. This hope is of very great importance. But too often the minor questions divide God's people into arguing and quibbling segments.

In a series of talks to a congregation I once presented the eschatological principles expressed in this book. There was good interest, but yet a number of empty seats. "If you'd announce that you were going to talk on what will happen during the tribulation period, this church would be full," the pastor told me.

69. What part will the angels have in the end events?

The drama of redemption is exciting because it recounts, from beginning to end, a great conflict, the battle of the ages. This battle is between the forces of good, led by Christ, and the forces of evil, led by Satan.

On both sides in this struggle are multitudes of spirit beings—innumerable angels, both of good and of evil. In his vision during the night Daniel saw one hundred million angels standing before the Ancient of Days (Daniel 7:10). The Bible mentions angels nearly three hundred times. However, there are more references to the holy angels than to the demons. They serve many functions, and are much involved in the end-time program.

Michael, the only one called an archangel (Jude 9), was involved in revealing the prophetic program of the ages to Daniel. At the last day Michael will blow the trumpet call. He leads the battle against the dragon in Revelation 12. Gabriel is mentioned more often in the announcement of good news. Unnamed angels often serve as messengers, like the ones who after the ascension promised that Jesus would return, and the angel of the apocalypse (Revelation 1:1).

Among the evil angels, Lucifer is another name for Satan, their chief.

Angels, like us, do not know when the end will come, but will be ready to play their assigned parts. They are subject to Christ (1 Peter 3:22).

At the parousia, all the mighty, holy angels will accompany Him. They will have the discernment to gather out all that is against Christ and His kingdom. They will participate in Armageddon, the last conflict between God's forces of good and Satan's world forces of darkness. That titanic battle will probably be waged by spirits rather than by political nations with military weapons.

Angels will be used as God's agents in judgment, as He used the destroying angel in Egypt. They will separate the sheep from the goats, the wheat from the chaff. They will throw the brambles into the fire. They will bind Satan with a chain, and throw him into a lake of fire with his evil followers (Matthew 25:41).

The multitude of angels will give to the coming of Jesus inexpressible brightness and glory. He is worthy of the holy worship and breathless adoration of that great celestial host. As the angels welcomed Jesus into the world with song at His first coming, so they will sing at the parousia tremendous hallelujahs and other great choruses of praise.

As the angels even now rejoice when one believer is added to the people of God, so their joy will swell a thousandfold when they see the multitudes of every tribe and tongue awarded their final salvation.

The evil angels are now reserved in judgment which awaits them for their disobedience and rebellion. They kept not their first estate (Jude 6), and so they shall be doomed to wander in darkness forever.

Through eternity, as even now, angels will be marveling spectators of the results of God's saving grace. They do not experience salvation as we can, but rejoice with us for its glorious reality. As Oatman and Sweney sang it years ago:

> Holy! Holy! Holy!
> Is what the angels sing;
> And I expect to help them
> Make the courts of glory ring.
>
> But when I sing redemption's story
> They will fold their wings,
> For angels never felt the joy
> That our salvation brings."

70. What is the power and the glory with which Christ will come?

One detail of description about the parousia is that Christ will ride on God's chariot, the clouds. That doesn't mean that He must come on a cloudy day, with one thunderhead chasing another across the sky. The clouds are symbols of heavenly majesty. This is the glory which belongs to Christ, before all time, and now, and for evermore. Jude (v. 25) further piles up the words, such as: "glory, majesty, dominion, and power." Luke (21:27) and Matthew (24:30) say He will come in great glory. In Mark's parallel verse (13:26) it is the power which is great. Paul says (2 Thessalonians 1:7-9) that He will come in the "glory of his might," and that the power will be manifested "in flaming fire."

Christ was willing to lay aside something of the glory which belonged to Him when He was clothed in flesh. In His first coming He was humiliated and rejected—spit upon, mocked, scourged, and crucified. But even in this ministry of shame His essential glory showed through in His transfiguration, and His power and authority was manifested again and again in His teachings and His miracles.

But only when He comes again will the sum of all His attributes shine forth in their total, splendid glory. Only at the end of this age will cosmic upheaval demonstrate His omnipotent power in dramatic triumph.

For His disciples Jesus prayed that they might behold His glory. After His resurrection He asked the two on the way to Emmaus whether they did not see that the Christ ought to enter into His glory. At the ascension He took His place of authority and power at the right hand of the Father. As we look forward to His second coming, we anticipate the glory which shall be revealed to us. And we are eager to realize the fullness of His power when He presents Himself to the world as the great God (Titus 2:3).

An Advent Song
(Written in a cotton field)

There's a King and Captain high, who'll be comin' by-and-by
And He'll find me hoein' cotton when He comes;
You will hear His legions chargin' in the thunders of the sky,
And He'll find me hoein' cotton when He comes!
    When He comes, when He comes,
All the dead will rise in answer to His drums,

While the fires of His encampment star the firmament on
  high,
And the heav'ns are rolled asunder, when He comes!
There's a Man they thrust aside, who was tortured till He
  died,
And He'll find me hoein' cotton when He comes;
He was hated and rejected, He was scourged and crucified,
But He'll find me hoein' cotton when He comes!
    When He comes, when He comes,
He'll be ringed with saints and angels when He comes;
They'll be shoutin' out hosanna to the Man that men
  denied,
And I'll kneel among my cotton when He comes.

—Author unknown

71. What is the normal attitude of the Christian regarding the second coming?

The caretaker of a country estate kept the premises
spic-and-span for the unpredictable visits of the owner
from the city. An observer said, "You act as if your
master were coming tomorrow."

"Today, sir, today," was the answer of the faithful
employee.

"Watch therefore: for ye know not on what day your
Lord cometh" (Matthew 24:42). And the longer the
waiting, the more we need to be told to watch.

To watch means to stay awake, to be aware that the
coming of Christ is due at any time. Paul linked together
"looking" and "living" (Titus 2:12, 13). Holy living is
expectant living. We expect Him to come, and the holiness of our lives shows our expectation.

We are unworldly people now because we are
constantly relating ourselves to the world which is to
come. Our hope and our obedience walk hand in hand.
We show that we expect a heavenly tomorrow by the

way we live today. We live so that we would not be embarrassed or surprised if He should come today. As the hour grows later, it is easy for believers to fall into the ways of this present world. But it should be normal for us to live as pilgrims bound for another land.

Such waiting should also involve us in active service for God and our fellowmen. Conscious of the future as we ought to be, we must never forget the present. A true eschatology is always a call to action. There are things to be done before Christ comes, and the fact that He may come at any time urges us to get to work. He must not find us idle. To be doing nothing is to be unprepared to meet Him.

Our chief responsibility is evangelization. Even though we see wickedness increase, it is our passion to preach the gospel to all. The Great Commission sets the program for this age. The gospel witness is our uncompleted assignment. Because Christ will come to the whole world, the fruit of the gospel must be gathered from all nations. Doing His work is the normal way to be watching for Him.

We must wait, also, in certain hope. We have emphasized our ignorance of when He will come. This must never drag us down into doubts as to whether He will come at all.

Can we be sure? How can we be certain of something that has not yet happened? On the basis of what has already happened. The end is even now in process. The first advent was the beginning of a series of events and developments which will go on to the second advent. The same plan and power which brought Him once cannot fail to bring Him again.

So we are not watching for something that may happen. We are waiting for the completion of something surely begun. So surely will it end as God has purposed.

Look at the parallel of lightning and thunder. Both come from the same discharge of electricity. When once the lightning has flashed, surely the thunder will roll. There is only the little period of waiting between.

The same God who invaded history in the incarnation will invade it again in the parousia. We live now in the land of promise. The city which we look for in that land is being built by the One who promised it. What He has promised and what He is doing He will not forsake. His whole project is a certain one. We watch for the project to come into fulfillment.

72. Why should the Christian continue to pray, "Maranatha"?

The word *maranatha* appears in 1 Corinthians 16:22. It is a phrase in Aramaic, the language of common speech at Jerusalem when the gospel had its beginning. *Mar* is the Aramaic for Lord. The early church believed in Jesus as divine Lord.

Atha means come. The whole phrase means either "Our Lord is coming" or "Our Lord, come." This Aramaic word was understood and used by Greek Christians, just as they used *amen, hosanna,* and *abba.*

The phrase was used in worship and became a watchword of Christian Jews and Greeks. They whispered it to each other in a language the pagans did not know. The imminent coming of the Lord was their vital hope.

Just as Jesus taught them to pray, "Thy kingdom come," so they prayed on any and every occasion, "Our Lord, come." In his first epistle to the Corinthians, Paul put into his salutation, in his own handwriting, this prayer: "Our Lord, come." The Apostle John brought his Revelation, and the whole body of the Scriptures, to a conclusion with the prayer, "Come, Lord Jesus" (Revelation 22:20).

Why should they, and why should we, continue to pray this prayer?

Because wrapped up in the creedal faith in Christ is a personal affection for Christ. "Lovest thou me?" was His question to Peter, as if that were more important than "What do you think about Me?" It is in the context of love that John speaks of the parousia of Christ. Paul speaks of those who love Christ's appearing.

The church, because it loves Christ, looks forward with eagerness to the day of meeting. The bride anticipates meeting the Bridegroom. It is a day to be desired, not dreaded. It is the wedding day, not the doomsday. The natural prayer of one who looks forward to a lovers' meeting is, "Come quickly, Lord Jesus, come."

Of course, there are other reasons for desiring and praying for Christ's coming. In the same text to the Corinthians, Paul uses another word right up against the prayer for Christ's coming. It is *anathema,* a word of curse or judgment. The anathema is on anyone who professes faith in Christ and has no love for Him.

Paul, eager to see truth and right triumphant, probably is praying that Christ may come to put an end to all strife and to all the activity of hostile forces in the church. He knows that Christ must come to bring His kingdom to its triumph, and to bring to full recognition the lordship of Jesus.

In this context, he writes, "We leave all evil men to the judgment of the Lord who is coming soon."

VII

The Hope of the Resurrection

73. Why was the resurrection of Christ a crucial event?

In the great climactic moment of the drama of redemption (see question 23), Jesus rose from the dead. This was a very important happening.

It was important for Jesus' disciples. They had expected Him to set up a kingdom—simply to assert His power, and the kingdom would become an immediate reality.

Instead He was executed, crucified as a common criminal. What a cruel disillusionment! "We thought He was the One!" they moaned.

And so the evidence of Easter day was good news. Sorrow turned suddenly into joy. Frustration made an about-face into confidence. "He is after all what He claimed to be and what we hoped He was."

It was an important event for the human race. Death had been the dread reality which all men feared. It was an enemy which always had the last word. Death was the effect of sin. Since sin was universal, there was no escape from this result. No one could get release from this penalty.

But in His resurrection Christ broke the stranglehold of death. Through Him life, not death, would prevail. In His life is the promise and assurance of life for all who believe in Him.

The heart of the early Christian message was the resurrection. The apostles were witnesses to what they saw and knew to be true. Upon this witness the church was built. Earliest Christianity consisted of the recital of a great event, the redemptive act of God in raising Jesus from the dead. Jesus is a living Savior.

The resurrection event created resurrection faith. The resurrection validated everything else the church believed about Christ. Resurrection faith became the foundation of the church.

Resurrection truth announced to the world a new order of life. The resurrection of Christ was an event in history. But it tells of a kind of life that belongs to the age to come. So it is eschatology. It reveals the consummation—in history, but beyond history—happening in this age, but demonstrating a kind of life which will become a reality in the age to come.

The resurrection of Christ, therefore, was an important event crowning Passion Week. It was at the same time a forecast of the resurrection of saints which will accompany the parousia. Christians would have no hope of being raised in the future if Christ had not risen in the past.

74. In what sense is Christ the firstborn from the dead?

In preaching the resurrection of Christ, the apostles Paul and John showed Christ as the first of many others who in God's plan should rise from the dead. First Christ, at the end of His incarnational ministry, then those who should follow Him, at the end of this age.

Acts 26:23. In his hearing before King Agrippa Paul admits preaching that Christ is the first to have died and risen again to life. By His resurrection Christ has brought light to His followers by overcoming death for them. At Christ's second coming others will share His victory over death. In that glorious hour those who have died will be raised to life, following the pattern and sharing the power of the risen Christ.

Colossians 1:18. In establishing the preeminence of Christ, Paul wrote to the Colossian Christians, as an illustration of this preeminence, that Christ began in His own resurrection what is to be shared at the parousia by all believers. At the end of the age the beginning He made will be the pattern which all His own shall follow.

1 Corinthians 15:20, 23. In his great treatment on the resurrection, Paul uses the language of the harvest. Before the main harvest comes the first sheaf, the firstfruits, a pledge and a sample of the coming harvest. The risen Christ is but the first of the great multitude who shall rise from the dead. Already there has been the resurrection of Christ, the type and pledge of the manifold defeat of death. The full celebration of this victory will come in the resurrection of His followers at His advent.

Revelation 1:5. John, in his introduction to the Book of Revelation, describes Jesus as the firstborn of the dead. Of all those who have gone the way of dusty death, Jesus is the first who rose from death to life. What about Lazarus and a few others in both Testaments who were miraculously restored to life? In a real resurrection the one raised never dies again. Jesus was resurrected, not only resuscitated or restored. When He was resurrected, death never again had any power over Him.

Because Christ the immortal arose as the firstfruits of

the resurrection, so we too shall experience a rising from the dead. But Christ leads that procession. As the firstborn, He has that place of honor and preeminence.

God has eternal purposes which He will fulfill for us in the Christ who was and is and is to come. May endless, living praise be His!

75. What is the redemption of the body?

A Christian husband and father had died, and his body lay in the casket. At the funeral the family stood around to look once more at the face of the one they loved so much.

"It isn't the last," said the mother. "you'll see him again." Most of the family were Christians, and shared their mother's belief in the resurrection of the body.

They knew that the body of Christ did not remain in the tomb furnished for it by Joseph of Arimathea. On Easter morning this tomb was found empty. The cloths which had been wrapped around the body of Jesus lay there, an empty chrysalis.

Jesus had been raised from the dead. Those who had known Him before recognized the Person they saw, even though there seemed to be some sense of strangeness. But whether it was in the garden, or in the house in Emmaus, or behind the locked doors in Jerusalem, or on the seashore in Galilee, they knew it was He. They saw His face and the wounds of His body. They heard the familiar intonations of His voice. He ate with them. For the few weeks before His ascension He had the power to reappear and disappear. Some hundreds gave witness to the resurrection of Jesus' body.

The Christian family mentioned above believed that the body of their loved one, about to be buried in the cemetery, would follow the pattern of Jesus' resurrection when Jesus comes again.

Then in some way that none of us knows enough to describe, this body in the casket will be changed by the miracle of God's power to a resurrection body. Incorruption will triumph over corruption, immortality over mortality, the spiritual over the material, perfection over imperfection, life over death. That will be the redemption of the body.

It is not enough that our souls be saved. We are whole persons, physical-spiritual beings, affected in our entirety by sin. We need to be totally redeemed, in body and soul. Our spiritual redemption, realized even now, will include our bodies in the day of resurrection.

In Paul's language, we are "waiting for . . . the redemption of our body" (Romans 8:23). This completed redemption is what we anticipate, and what God has promised.

76. Will the unsaved experience bodily resurrection?

Jesus said, "For the hour cometh, in which all that are in the tombs shall hear his voice, and shall come forth; they that have done good, unto the resurrection of life; and they that have done evil, unto the resurrection of life; and they that have done evil, unto the resurrection of judgment" (John 5:28, 29). Both the good and the evil, all who have died, shall be raised. This is the clear teaching of the Bible.

Paul's letters were addressed to Christian people, and so his teachings on the resurrection were chiefly on the resurrection of saints. But we must not think that he did not teach a universal resurrection. He argued before

Felix "a resurrection both of the just and unjust" (Acts 24:15).

The unsaved will stand before God's judgment throne in resurrected bodies. They will experience the resurrection, not of redemption, but of eternal judgment.

The resurrection of all mankind is an essential part of the basic eschatology of the New Testament. Whatever else we believe or do not believe and teach about eschatology, this we must accept: Jesus will return, the dead will be raised, all will be judged. If we accept the scriptures as the Word of God, we must accept the parousia, the resurrection, and the judgment as the minimal framework of the last things.

According to one interpretation of Revelation 20:5, all of the dead may not be raised at the same time. But that does not affect the answer to our question as to whether the unsaved will be resurrected.

77. Which is it: immortality or resurrection?

Paul was at Athens, the intellectual capital of the Greek and Roman world. Before him in the Areopagus stood the brainy Epicurean and Stoic philosophers, the successors of Socrates, Plato, and Aristotle. They listened to Paul with interest and tolerance, until he told them of a Person who was raised from the dead after He had been crucified.

Such an idea amused the philosophers. Thinkers that they were, they couldn't believe in the possibility of the resurrection of a dead body.

They did believe in the immortality of the soul. Plato had taught them that the body is evil and mortal. The soul, the noble part of man, is immortal. Death sets the soul free from the evil encumbrance of the body, the philosophers thought. Whoever would want his dead body to be raised?

And so they laughed! They believed in immortality, but not in resurrection. The Egyptians, too, believed in life after death. Hinduism believes in the transmigration of souls. The American Indians believed in a happy hunting ground.

But resurrection is a Christian teaching. It is based on the historic action of Christ. It is one of the clearest teachings of the New Testament. Jesus prophesied His own resurrection, and that of all mankind. After Pentecost the apostles "proclaimed in Jesus the resurrection from the dead" (Acts 4:2). In Paul's epistles, particularly, it is set forth as the specifically Christian doctrine.

One Christian mortician says he seldom hears a funeral sermon about the resurrection. Many of us have become more Greek than Christian in our thinking. Resurrection has come to mean only immortality. D. T. Niles tells us: "Man is not an immortal soul in a mortal body. Man is body and soul—a total person in an immortal relationship to God."

Death breaks a unity which must be restored by a resurrection of the body. The Christian doesn't want to get rid of his body as something evil. He wants to have it redeemed by the same power that raised Jesus from the dead.

How will the dead be raised? It will be a miracle, of course, and we can leave its working to God. The mortal body, says Paul in 1 Corinthians 15, is the seed to which the spiritual resurrection body is related. The resurrection body will be like the postresurrection body of Christ. The resurrection of Christ gives us hope in a world of death.

78. At death, where does one's spirit go?

Yesterday I attended a funeral. A dead body lay in a casket, and an open grave waited in the cemetery. Relatives and friends had gathered in loving and respectful memory. The minister in charge of the service read an obituary of the "departed." Where had she gone?

The Bible has something to say in answer to that question, but not very much. We don't need much information on this. Most of what could be told us we would not understand, for it is about a country never seen by our eyes, about a culture we have never experienced.

What we most need to know is how to prepare for the next life. God has told us all we need to know about it. What we will experience beyond death we can see when we get there.

It is not the final destination of heaven or hell that our question asks about. Coming next on the program are the parousia of Christ, the resurrection, and the judgment. After the verdict of judgment come the final destinies. And that will be the end of this age.

Where are our departed loved ones now, before that end time comes. And where will we go, if death's call comes before that of the archangel? Many have already been in that intermediate place or condition for a long, long time. One answer from the Scriptures is that given by Jesus to the thief who asked to be remembered in Christ's kingdom. "Today thou shalt be with me in Paradise" (Luke 23:43). Where is that?

Paradise is a New Testament term for a beautiful garden. It was a place where the blessed dead were at rest in a dwelling of God. So the righteous dead are at home with God.

Paul spoke of seeing wonderful things in Paradise (2

Corinthians 12:3, 4). He said he was eager to be with Christ (Philippians 1:23), "absent from the body and . . . at home with the Lord" (2 Corinthians 5:8).

Stephen, as he was being martyred, prayed, "Lord Jesus, receive my spirit" (Acts 7:59).

So the dead who are saved are with Jesus. There they are safe in peace and rest and joy and glory.

There are passages which speak of death as a sleep, and some think this is an unconscious sleep. But it is more likely a figure of speech, the sleeper actually being conscious. How could one unconsciously be with Christ?

There is no clear scriptural evidence for purgatory, a Catholic doctrine of suffering after death to make atonement for one's sins. That would not be salvation by grace.

The Old Testament speaks of all the dead going to Sheol. This is a place of silence and darkness, where the shades are gathered. It is not so much a place as the state of death. There is no clear teaching in the Old Testament of a blessed intermediate state. But the germ of the idea appears, in that even death cannot break one's communion with God. For instance: "And I shall dwell in the house of Jehovah for ever" (Psalms 23:6).

Sheol is not a place of punishment. Sheol testifies that death does not terminate human existence. Sheol in New Testament times became Hades, sometimes translated "hell" in English. The intermediate condition of lostness is now the beginning of separation from God.

79. What happens to the believers still living at the parousia?

Paul's earliest writing on the parousia was to the

Thessalonians. Paul had taught these Christian believers "to wait for his Son from heaven" (1 Thessalonians 1:10).

But since then Timothy had reported that some of the believers at Thessalonica had died. They had not been able to wait until Christ came again. How did this affect their hope in Christ?

And what could those still alive expect to happen when Christ came for them? They needed some more instruction from the apostle, which he gave in the first epistle he wrote to them (4:13—5:11).

First he tells them that those who have died will experience a resurrection. As spirits they went to be with Christ when they died, and Christ will bring them with Him at the parousia. Their bodies will be raised from the dead, and their spirits and their resurrection bodies will be united. They will meet the Lord in the air. That is one pattern, then, for this age: death, the parousia, resurrection and being united with Christ.

But because the parousia will come before some of His believers die and take this course, what will happen to them when Christ does return? They too need the change into resurrection bodies.

First the dead shall be changed as they are resurrected. Then as Paul later wrote in 1 Corinthians 15:51, 52, those who are still living will be changed. Thus they will bypass the experience of death and burial and will undergo resurrection-like change, after the manner of those who died and rose again. Those going the route of death will lose nothing. And those bypassing the resurrection experience will be at no disadvantage. "And we shall thus always"—and all of us—" be with the Lord" (1 Thessalonians 4:17, NEB).

80. What intermediate state may we expect?

Church hymnals include hymns on the "communion of saints." This phrase comes from the ancient Apostles' Creed. Through the centuries the Christian church has believed that God's people on both sides of death are united in the same faith and interests and concerns.

One of these hymns is by Charles Wesley:

> Let saints on earth unite and sing,
>   With those to glory gone;
> For all the servants of our King,
>   In earth and heav'n, are one.
>
> One family we dwell in Him,
>   One church above, beneath,
> Though now divided by the stream,
>   The narrow stream of death.

Communication between the two sides of this fellowship, those in Christ before death and those with Christ in the intermediate state before the resurrection at the coming of Christ, is very meager. Some people before the hour of death have had little glimpses across the border about which they could tell us: faces which they recognized, voices, music of a heavenly quality, lovely sights and colors, and an atmosphere of peace and joy. Some who were called back from the border to stay here have been sorry to return to the pains and mists of earth.

Numerous stories have been told, which may be authentic, of persons who came back to tell us something from the other side. Here, however, we must guard against demonic lies of spiritism.

The New Testament gives us some light:

On the Mount of Transfiguration Moses and Elijah came out of invisibility to talk with Jesus about His coming passion experiences.

Jesus told the story of Lazarus and the rich man communicating across the gulf which separated the peace of Abraham's bosom and the torment of Hades.

Jesus, during the interval between His death and His resurrection, preached to the spirits in prison (1 Peter 3:19).

Paul shrank from disembodied nakedness as he anticipated waiting after death for his resurrection body (2 Corinthians 5:2-4). Paul listed death and things to come as not being able to defeat the love of God in him (Romans 8:38).

Jesus described Abraham as being glad, hundreds of years after his death, that the time of Christ's redemptive ministry had come (John 8:56).

What we may expect between death and resurrection:

—God with us in the hour of death (Psalm 23:4).
—Angels to usher us from the darkness below to the light above (Luke 16:22).
—The constant presence of Christ (2 Corinthians 5:8).
—Disembodied conscious existence (2 Corinthians 5:8).
—Living parallel to earthly existence and conscious of it.
—Recognizing those gone before and enjoying reunion with them.
—Continuation of the same personality.
—No place for repentance and accepting God's mercy.
—Enjoying the reality of salvation and redemption.
—Growth in the fullness of personhood.
—Praising and worshiping in greater freedom and perfection.
—Looking forward to perfect redemption and resurrection bodies at Christ's coming.
—Seeing past and present at true value.
—"Mystic sweet communion with those whose rest is won."

VIII
The Ultimate Judgment

81. What divine judgments are already past or now in process?

Which direction are you looking when you think of judgment—forward or backward? Probably forward: it is an event which we expect in the future.

But judgment started long ago. The Bible is full of it from Genesis to Revelation. God judged sin in Eden, in the Flood, in the destruction of Sodom, in the plagues of Egypt. He judged Israel in the several captivities, in the utter destruction of Jerusalem, and in a dispersion of the Jews through the centuries. Judgment is seen in a whole series of national calamities, such as Babylon, Alexander's Greece, the Roman Empire, Hitler's Germany. We see God's judgment in the way war and man's greed desolate the earth. God's hand of judgment is manifest throughout the course of history.

Though Jesus was sent to be the world's savior, He said that all judgment had been committed to Him (John 5:22). His very presence created a judgment scene. Wherever He was, the court was in session. Evil persons felt condemned as they stood or sat or walked before Him.

Then, and since then, the fate of individuals has turned upon their reaction to the person and the mission of Jesus. When they reject Him and refuse to follow His ways, they feel condemnation. Already they are judged by Him. Judgment, although it has an eschatological prospect, is even now a present reality.

Our consciences are constantly pronouncing judgment, accusing us of wrong conduct, and approving when we follow Christ. The final judgment will simply confirm the decision of conscience. The judgment we already experience will only be intensified and finalized when Jesus returns.

On the cross Jesus faced God's judgment against sin. The awfulness of what happened there is a testimony to what God thinks and feels about the sinfulness of mankind. Sin made it necessary for the Son to take upon Himself human flesh, like a common criminal to be tortured and crucified, to suffer in agony and to die as an atonement for sin. Behold, what sin has done, says the Father as He accepts this tremendous sacrifice.

As we confess our sinfulness, we are judging ourselves to be violaters of God's laws, and deserving of death. But by faith we plead the death of Christ in our stead. God justified us because we have accepted His judgment of our sin, and His way of salvation through Christ. Judgment and salvation are two sides of the same coin.

Living as followers of Christ requires that we judge the walk of sin as wrong and unacceptable for the Christian. Every day we measure our lives by the standards of righteousness as seen in Christ, and count ourselves dead to these ways of sin. Thus our justification by God is complemented by a holiness of life which is oriented to divine judgment.

82. What is the purpose of the final judgment?

"From thence [heaven] He shall come to judge the quick and the dead."

Thus the Apostles' Creed affirms the belief of the Christian church that there will be a judgment when Christ returns at the end of this age. He will come; He will come to judge; He will judge all of us, the living and the dead.

The second advent is tied to the judgment. And because the dead will be judged, the resurrection is also tied to the judgment.

Some judgments, we have seen, are past. But there is a future judgment—a "day when God shall judge" (Romans 2:16). The New Testament clearly teaches such a judgment which cannot be escaped. It will be a single event: a day (Acts 17:31), the day (2 Peter 3:7). The narrow pass of judgment is the location of the gate between the here and the hereafter.

This time, called in both Testaments the day of the Lord, is the sudden, unexpected, inescapable, and imminent coming of the Lord in judgment.

This judgment is necessary because all people are accountable to God. In the judgment they give account. If there is no accounting, then decision and action are not important. Judgment underlines the choices we have made. Responsibility is an essential part of human personality. It is God's right to hold us responsible. There is a moral need for a squaring of accounts.

Have we said yes or no to Christ? The judgment gives finality to our answer. And how have we treated other people, Christ's little ones? What has been our response to the will of God? In the judgment the "Son of man . . . shall render unto every man according to his deeds" (Matthew 16:27). Some will be condemned because they have given only lip service. The judgment will show us up for what we really are.

The root idea in judgment is discrimination and separation. The sheep will be separated from the goats, the wheat from the weeds. Jesus taught that full differentiation must await a final judgment, when all the evidence is in. Our human standards, apart from God's insights, are quite imperfect. There will be surprises. God will judge the secrets of our hearts (Romans 2:16).

Much that is wrong in this world needs to be set right, much confusion needs to be put in order, much error must be exposed to God's truth. Man cannot render righteous judgment. God must do that. And He will, when Christ sits in judgment at His coming. "Shall not the Judge of all the earth do right?" (Genesis 18:25).

For those of us who have accepted God's judgment of our sins in the cross of Christ, the day of judgment has lost its terror. We are persuaded that in Christ we have salvation. We are aware that in the judgment our works shall be judged, and our record may not be as good as we had hoped it would be (1 Corinthians 3:12-15). But we look forward to the judgment without fear, assured that even though our reward for works may be small, we ourselves shall be saved in Christ.

83. How will the judgment be conducted?

"There ain't no throne, and there ain't no books,
    It's 'Im you've got to see."

That's how Studdert-Kennedy's cockney tells what the judgment will be like. All the people who ever lived will be there for that trial. But it isn't such an unnumbered throng that impresses him. It isn't the glorious throne surrounded by angels and archangels. It isn't any vast machinery of charges and testimony and defense.

All that the cockney sees is the Judge, silently looking him in the eyes. And all that the silence says is, "Well?" We will not need to hear any charges. We will know how we stand before that omnipotent Judge.

Then the full and awful meaning of Hebrews 4:13 will be clear to us: "There is no creature that is not manifest in his sight: but all things are naked and laid open before the eyes of him with whom we have to do."

"It comes to light." This is the essence of judgment. Not to God—for He has known everything about us all along. But to us: before Him we are exposed to the truth of our being. There will be no need of documents. The books that are opened will be the books of our own memories. We shall judge ourselves, just as the evil-hearted old scribes and Pharisees did when Jesus stood silent before them.

This explains how such a multitude can be judged, all at the same time. John Wesley, thinking in terms of our court hearings, figured that the judgment would take thousands of years. But it will not be such a long-drawn-out calendar of cases.

Our Judge will be the same person who came to be our Savior. The same holiness and truth and love and understanding will be in evidence. He will simply be bringing to its full completion the judgment which He exercised before and is exercising now. The conclusions of that court will be totally righteous, just, and fair. No one will question the decisions or feel a need for appeal.

At this final judgment the salvation of God's people is not at issue. For them their works are to be judged. The book of life and the book of works are cross-referenced. We shall be judged for our obedience and faithfulness, for the thoughts and intents of our hearts, for the use and abuse of opportunity. The ultimate worth of a person's life and work will stand for or against him, for reward or for loss. Reward shall be proportioned to the measure of service, and loss to the measure of failure.

All will be judged by deepest principles, and not by superficialities. Opportunity and capacity will be taken into consideration. So there must be degrees of punishment and reward. Those who suffer ultimate loss will perish by their own fault and deliberate choice.

The judgment will vindicate the holiness and righteousness of God.

84. What is eternal life and eternal death?

"This is the end. For me, the beginning of life." These were the last words of Dietrich Bonhoeffer, the German pastor, before his execution by the Nazis in 1945.

Life is for the Christian something that physical death, even though it be a tragic one like Bonhoeffer's, cannot interrupt. But was he right in saying that eternal life would have its beginning only when life left his body? That is not what the New Testament, especially the Gospel of John, means by eternal life.

The Old Testament contains the idea that God has life, and that He gives life to humanity. This is chiefly biological life. In the teaching of the rabbis life beyond this physical existence belonged to the age to come. Only in the future, when the Messiah appeared, or perhaps after the resurrection at the end of this age, would anyone experience eternal life.

The first three Gospels use eternal life only with this meaning. For instance, Jesus told His disciples that if they give up much for the kingdom now, they will receive "in the world to come eternal life" (Luke 18:30).

With John, eternal life becomes the central theme of Jesus' teaching. The idea of eschatological life is continued, as in John 12:25. Here eternal life is the enjoyment of fellowship with God in the age to come.

But the majority of dozens of uses of *life* speak to a present eternal life. It was the purpose of Jesus' mission to give us a present experience of the future life. (John 10:10). He came to satisfy, now, the world's spiritual hunger and thirst (John 6:35).

So there is a frequent connection between the present reception and experience of life and the future enjoyment of that life (John 5:25). Thus our Lord wedded the present and the future in an unbreakable bond. The life that belongs to the new age has already come in this old age. In the present life in Christ's kingdom we have a wonderful foretaste of the life of the future age.

Eternal life involves the resurrection of the body. Since believers already have this life in Christ, they will never die. Yes, they die physically, but they will live again at the last day.

Eternal life is imparted through Christ as a matter of personal experience. Christ's followers meet Him and come to know Him. They hear His words and believe them. They acknowledge that Christ is the Son of God and has come to bring salvation and life. They commit themselves to Jesus as Savior and Lord and take up the cross of obedience. They eat the bread of life and drink the water of life. They find Christ to be indeed the way, the truth, and the life. They have eternal life, and grow in their experience of that reality.

In the age to come they will live the same life, but in their resurrection bodies. To be with Christ is to come into a fuller, growing experience of eternal life. We shall know Christ better there than we can know Him here. We shall understand truth which we can but dimly perceive in this present age.

The word "eternal" does have a meaning of time in it. Forever and ever we shall sing praises to the source of our life.

But the quality of eternal life is more important than its quantity. Even now we experience the "riches of the glory of his inheritance in the saints" (Ephesians 1:18). In the ages to come He will progressively "show the exceeding riches of his grace in kindness toward us in Christ Jesus" (Ephesians 2:7).

Eternal death is the opposite of eternal life. God has set before us "life and death, good and evil" (Deuteronomy 30:15), "the way of life and the way of death" (Jeremiah 21:8). Those who refuse the life which Christ offers "abide in death" (1 John 3:14). They shall find that "the wages of sin is death" (Romans 6:23). By their own choice they shall be without the privileges and blessings which adorn those who live in Christ.

Dietrich Bonhoeffer might better have said, "This is the end of what Hitler can do to me. It will bring to fuller development the life which I have begun to live in Christ."

85. Who is the antichrist, and what will happen to him?

The antichrist is a mysterious Bible personage of the end time. He is a hell-bound embodiment of antagonism to God's law. The very essence of his character is lawlessness. This great blasphemer will be inspired by Satan to persecute God's people as the advent of Christ approaches. He is a rival Christ.

Daniel called him the little horn and pictured him as a great personage of rebellion (Daniel 8:9-11). Jesus said that false Christs would come (Matthew 24:24). Paul prophesied that the man of lawlessness would be destroyed at the coming of Christ (2 Thessalonians 2:8). John said that there are already many antichrists in the world (1 John 4:3). The beast of Revelation 13 has the same anti-God qualities as the man of lawlessness.

What will the antichrist do?

He will try to dethrone God and enthrone himself (2 Thessalonians 2:3, 4).

He will demand worship and total submission (Revelation 13:7, 8).

He will be empowered by Satan to deceive people and turn them from the truth (2 Thessalonians 2:9, 10).

He will set himself in violent opposition to God.

He will be supported by a general rebellion against God.

He will deify a demonic, totalitarian state (Revelation 13).

His rule of law will break down, and lawless chaos will follow.

This short period of terrible evil will be terminated by the return of Christ.

The antichrist will be suddenly and decisively destroyed by the manifestation of Christ's coming (2 Thessalonians 2:8). It is this fact which dates him at the time of the end.

He will be cast into the lake of fire with Satan and the false prophet (Revelation 20:10).

Who is the antichrist? Probably a person of the end time, although some think that the term is applied to a system or a series of persons (like the popes).

Many attempts have been made to identify the antichrist. The number 666 (Revelation 13:18) has been a chief clue.

There have been many guesses: Domitian (the emperor who sent John the Revelator to Patmos), Cerinthus, Titus (the Roman emperor who destroyed Jerusalem), Luther (a Roman Catholic guess), Napoleon, Mussolini, Nietsche, Hitler, Stalin. I have been expecting someone to guess that he'll be an Arab or to name Idi Amin!

Any powerful person on the political or religious scene may be called the antichrist by contemporaries who oppose him. For instance, the introduction to the King James translation said that James, king of England, was dealing a blow to the papal antichrist by authorizing this translation.

If we get too much absorbed in who the antichrist is, we may fall into some evil system which is against Christ, and fail to recognize how we are deceived.

The anti-Christian principle was at work in the times of the apostles. Satan has worked ever since in evil persons and wicked governments. The teachings about the Antichrist indicate that all wickedness will come to a head just before the end of the age. We can trust the Lord to keep us from its terrors.

But it is good to know that Christ's coming will bring the embodiment of all evil to defeat. Tyranny, persecution, corruption, and rebellion will be no more. The Messiah's very breath will be enough to destroy the lawless one and all who follow his way. The pompous claims of the antichrist will come to an inglorious end. Then Christ will be Kings of kings and Lord of lords. Christ, not Satan, will have the last word.

86. What is the "wrath of God"?

God loves us. This the Christian must believe. God's very nature is love (1 John 4:16). When He loves He is truly expressing Himself. He loved the creatures He made to live and work with Him on earth. When man sinned, God so loved that He provided redemption for him by giving His own Son. There can be no question of God's love.

But frequently we also read in the Bible of God's wrath. This is the most vivid term for describing the divine reaction to human rebellion and disobedience. Sinners are called children of wrath. The wrath of God comes upon the sons of disobedience (Colossians 3:6).

The chief focus of this wrath is eschatological. The day of wrath (Romans 2:5) is the day of judgment, which is the "wrath to come" (1 Thessalonians 1:10). Paul says that at the revelation of the Lord Jesus He will render "vengeance to them that know not God" (2 Thessalonians 1:8).

But we already are described as being by nature the "the children of wrath" (Ephesians 2:3). Our sinful natures have impelled us to live in ways that displease God and offend His holy will. For this God must condemn us, both now and in the future judgment. However, "God appointed us not unto wrath, but unto the obtaining of salvation" (1 Thessalonians 5:9).

What kind of God is this? Does He lose His temper and do and say things that he regrets? Does He have to ask our pardon when He flies off the handle with us?

Revelation 6 contains a great passage on the wrath, not of a lion, but a lamb. Here people of the earth ask the rocks to fall on them and to hide them from the Lamb, whose day of wrath has come. The Greek word for wrath here is not a feeling or emotion which God has. It is rather the universal, abiding opposition of God to every evil.

Wrath is not, then, how God feels, but how God acts toward sin. Sin is no trivial matter. Divine wrath expresses what God is doing and will do. In wrath the nature of God speaks quite as much as it does in His love. In fact, divine love and wrath are two sides of the same coin. God's wrath is the necessary agony of His love.

Those who have turned their backs on God's love, despised His forgiveness, and rejected His way are meeting in His wrath their own choices. It is God's love that permits them a choice.

> That day of wrath, that dreadful day,
> When heav'n and earth shall pass away!
> What power shall be the sinner's stay?
> How shall he meet that dreadful day?
>
> O on that day, that wrathful day,
> When man to judgment wakes from clay,
> Be Thou, O Christ, the sinner's stay,
> Tho' heav'n and earth shall pass away."
>   —*Thomas of Celano,* 13th century
>   Sir Walter Scott, translator

87. How does the Bible describe hell?

"What did you preach about yesterday?" one pastor asked another as they met on Monday morning.

"I preached about hell," was the answer.

"Brother! Did you do it with tears in your eyes?"

The doctrine of eternal separation from God has the undeniable support of Scripture. Jesus Himself said the most about hell, and the faithful preacher must not bypass the subject. But hell is a terrible place, and no one dare write or talk about it with a vindictive spirit. Hell is provided as an abode for the devil and his angels (Matthew 25:41). When people insist on going there too, it is cause for dreadful sorrow. Talk about hell with a broken voice. It is an awful word to use profanely.

Going to hell is the same as being lost, perishing, experiencing eternal death. Not to be saved is to lose one's life, and everything with it (Luke 9:25). Lostness is in the present tense, but it continues into the future.

The essence of hell is exclusion from the presence of God, and from the eternal enjoyment of His blessings. Those who choose to be godless are doomed to remain godless. The only alternative left them is to be with Satan.

This in itself is punishment. But hell is also a place of torment (Revelation 20:10). "Our God is a consuming fire" (Hebrews 12:29). Hell provides immortality, but without salvation. It is lostness without relief.

Hades is the abode of the dead—all the dead before the judgment. It is not hell, although some translations have called it that. The usual name for hell is "gehenna." Twelve times this word is used in the Greek New Testament. It comes from the Vale of Hinnom, which was the trash yard of Jerusalem. It was a foul place always reeking with decay and burning. It became a symbol of the everlasting abode of the wicked. It meant that to Jewish writers of the apocalypses, and Jesus uses the word with the same meaning. He spoke of the hell whose fire is not quenched. Gehenna is the abode of the lost, after the judgment.

Hell is described as a place of both fire and darkness. These are both effective metaphors for the indescribable. What fuel feeds the fire, and how does darkness burn? We can leave those engineering problems to someone who knows. The way electricity works may give us some hints. But we should avoid forcing materialistic concepts into spirit realms.

Hell is away from the face of God, who is light. It is down in a bottomless pit, where it is dark. Being with God is within; separated from God is without. Away from the light of heaven is in the darkness of hell.

Hell has been an attractive subject for the world's artists. Dante, a great Italian poet, wrote the *Inferno,* a whole book, about hell. He placed over the gate of hell these words: "Abandon hope, all ye who enter here." Here is a bit of the horror that he has imagined:

> They smote each other not alone with hands
> But with the head, and with the hands and feet,
> Tearing each other piecemeal with their teeth.

The translator of the Berkeley New Testament has this footnote on Mark 9:48: "Everlasting self-accusation, with no chance or desire to try again."

Hell's most dreadful torment must be the realization that they knew the way to heaven, but rejected it.

It is a mystery how the love of God can permit a hell. He doesn't send anyone there. But in all love there is a fire.

C. S. Lewis, in *The Great Divorce,* makes clear that the worst rape of personality would be sending someone to heaven who didn't want to go there.

88. What is the tragedy of going into eternity against God?

One of the most tragic characters of history is Judas Iscariot. His was a character of great promise. Jesus saw enough in him to call him to His inner circle of twelve disciples. He invested in these Twelve the training and the opportunity which was to make them the twelve apostles.

Judas had the personality and the talent of administration which gave him the call to be treasurer of the group. Jesus wished to make him a leader in the early church. He evidently had the potential to become a preacher or a writer or an executive of some sort. His name could have been attached to the record for honorable service for which we know Peter, James, and John.

Instead, he became an infamous traitor. Some motive made him sell his Master to a shameful death. When he tried to stop the tragic train of events, and failed, he died a horrible death on the Field of Blood. Jesus had to call him the son of perdition (John 17:12). He became a supreme example of lostness. What did he lose?

He lost the approval of the Lord Jesus. The Master had to name him as the one of twelve disciples disloyal enough to betray Him.

He lost eternal salvation. To be lost is not to be saved. Not to be saved is to die eternally.

He lost heaven, the privilege of standing before the face of the Father, of extending into endless ages his fellowship with the Son.

He lost peace of soul to a degree that drove him to hang himself from the limb of a tree.

He lost all hope for the future. God has given no inkling of another chance beyond the bounds of physical death.

He lost a career of pleasure and joy in effective service in the church of Christ.

He lost his place of reputation as one of the original twelve princes of the church. Did you ever know of anyone naming a son Judas? Judas Maccabeus lived before him.

He lost an opportunity to come into glory trailed by hundreds converted through his testimony.

Judas demonstrated for time and eternity the tragic effects of being for ages the enemy of God, carrying the awful burden of God's judgment.

God planned only good things for Judas Iscariot. He didn't intend for him to be the son of perdition. Could anything be more tragic than such a missing of God's purpose?

89. How does the Bible describe heaven?

"They shall see his face" (Revelation 22:4).

"And we shall be like him; for we shall see him even as he is" (1 John 3:2).

Jesus told His disciples He was going to prepare a place for them. So heaven is a place; where it is, we are not told.

But then Jesus said He would come back to receive His disciples, not to that place, but to Himself. That is the essence of heaven: the presence of God's people, face-to-face with God. "The tabernacle of God is with men, and he shall dwell with them, and they shall be his peoples, and God himself shall be with them, and be their God" (Revelation 21:3).

To provide that kind of a heaven, an eternal habitation of the saved, is the purpose and goal of God's plan of redemption.

We know enough about heaven to be sure of it. But we can't understand just what it will be like, for it will be different from anything we know. For instance, gold streets that look like pure glass. The reality of heaven will be better than the symbols which attempt to describe it to us.

It will be a large place, a fifteen-hundred-mile cube (Revelation 21:16). There will be room for all!

It will be a place of joy and comfort, light and rest. This is Dante's picture of it in the *Paradiso:* "It seemed like the laughter of the universe." There shall be healing for every torn emotion.

Some experiences we shall not have there: tears and sorrow, pain, hunger, and thirst. Tragic disabilities will be forgotten forever.

There will be no sin there—what a cause for rejoicing! And no other kind of imperfection (Revelation 21:27). Righteousness and total justice will prevail (2 Peter 3:13).

Jesus said that in our resurrection bodies there would be no marriage. The relationships of heaven transcend those of earth. God must have provided something better.

The supreme activity of heaven will be praise. The hallelujahs will never cease. All the activity will be worshipful. There will be music—singing and playing. It will be heavenly music, a new song (Revelation 14:3). The songs we sing on earth practically all infer some earthly situation.

There will be other spiritual and aesthetic delights. The architectural symmetry, the foundations of precious stones, the gates of pearl, the fruit trees bordering the crystal bright river—these must be symbolic of all sorts of heavenly glory and beauty, such as we have no way to sense now. Heaven will say yes to every good creation of God. It will be better than the best we can know here. Don't be troubled by the symbolism. Everything will be more solid and real than the materialism of earth.

There will be nothing boring in heaven. We shall have

greater things to do, in more variety. We shall have full ability and facility to explore the boundless reaches of grace, truth, and reality. We shall see the top side of the designs we have wondered about from beneath. What we will like to do, we shall be privileged to do. How could heaven have less to interest us than earth does? Nor need we know everything from the start. We can grow in understanding, even in heaven.

Since we shall reign in heaven (Revelation 22:5), we shall share responsibility. This will give us opportunity to show love in caring (1 Corinthians 13:12, 13).

Personal relationships will bless us in heaven. We shall still be persons, and shall know each other on a deeper level. There will be endless opportunity to fellowship with loved ones and with saints of other days. Make a list of those you would like to talk to, in addition to Jesus.

Heaven is God's home, and His welcome to us will be, "Make yourself at home." We shall put down our roots and settle in our mansions (John 14:2). Then we shall be "at home with the Lord" (2 Corinthians 5:8).

90. What is God's culminating purpose for human personality?

An English catechism puts the same question this way, "What is the chief end of man?" The answer is, "To know God and enjoy him fully forever."

Psalm 73 enlarges on this answer. The psalmist first observes how the wicked seem to be rewarded by health and wealth. The writer is entangled in despairing doubts. For it seems that keeping a heart pure toward God has done him no good. What did he get out of it?

Truth dawns on him when he comes into the

sanctuary of God. He considers the horrible end of the wicked apart from God, and the eternal blessings of God's people with Him. He sees that throughout life God will hold and guide him. And afterward God will receive him into glory. His life in the present is good. But it will have an "afterward" which will be better. While those who are far from God will perish, God will be the strength and joy of His people forever.

The psalmist sees, therefore, that God's purposes for him are served by his being near to God (v. 28). He is drawn near to God when he comes to the sanctuary to worship. Also when he is true to the traditions and teachings of God's children (v. 15). In all of this he has a sense of being continually in God's presence (v. 23).

There is, however, an eschatology in the purposes of God. The psalmist expects a welcome in another world or age (v. 24). His being with God in heaven is at the heart of his desire (v. 25). "Having thee, I desire nothing else on earth." And when his flesh and heart may fail in death, he knows that God will be his strength and possession in glory forever (v. 26).

God's culminating purpose for humankind is that all should be His people, fully and finally redeemed from the sins and imperfections of earth and time. He desires that the earth-course of each one of us should lead to the city of God, where we can enter into the joys of the Lord. The sovereign God does not intend to live alone in eternity, but face-to-face with those He has created and redeemed. He has planned nothing beyond that, for nothing could be better than such fellowship between Creator and creature. Nothing but the refusal of the creature can interfere with these ultimate plans for men.

BIBLIOGRAPHY

Banks, Robert, Ed., *Reconciliation and Hope.* Grand Rapids, Mich.: Eerdmans, 1974

Belk, Fred Richard, *The Great Trek.* Scottdale, Pa.: Herald Press, 1976 (but see Waldemar Janzen, "The Great Trek: Episode or Paradigm?" in *Mennonite Quarterly Review,* April, 1977)

Clouse, Robert G., *The Meaning of the Millennium.* Downers Grove, Ill.: Inter-Varsity Press, 1977

Culp, G. Richard, *Bible Studies in Prophecy.* Seymour, Mo.: Historical Mennonite Faith Publishers, 1971

DeCaro, Louis A., *Israel Today: Fulfillment of Prophecy—* Philadelphia, Pa.: Presbyterian and Reformed Publishing Company, 1974

Epp, Frank H., *The Palestinians.* Scottdale, Pa.: Herald Press, 1976

Epp, Theodore H., *Why Must Jesus Come Again?* Lincoln, Neb.: Back to the Bible Publishers, 1960

Erb, Paul, *The Alpha and the Omega.* Scottdale, Pa.: Herald Press, 1955, o.p.

Graham, Billy, *Angels.* Garden City, N.Y.: Doubleday, 1975

Grier, W. J., *The Momentous Event.* London: The Banner of Truth Trust, 1970

Hanson, Richard S., *The Future of the Great Planet.* Minneapolis, Minn.: Augsburg Publishing House, 1972

Hendriksen, William, *The Bible on the Life Hereafter.* Grand Rapids, Mich.: Baker Book House, 1975

Katterjohn, Arthur, *The Tribulation People.* Carol Stream, Ill.: Creation House, 1976

Kik, J. Marcellus, *An Eschatology of Victory.* Presbyterian and Reformed Publishing Company, 1975

Kraus, C. Norman, *Dispensationalism in America.* Richmond, Va.: John Knox Press, 1958

Ladd, George E., *The Presence of the Future.* Grand Rapids, Mich.: Eerdmans, 1974

——————, *A Theology of the New Testament.* Grand Rapids, Mich.: Eerdmans, 1974

La Sor, William S., *Israel*. Grand Rapids, Mich.: Eerdmans, 1976

Lehman, Chester K., *The Fulfillment of Prophecy*. Herald Press, 1971

Lilje, Hanns, *The Last Book of the Bible*. Philadelphia, Pa.: Muhlenberg Press, 1957

Lindsay, Hal, *The Terminal Generation*. Old Tappan, N.J.: Revell, 1976

Lockyer, Herbert, *All the Messianic Prophecies of the Bible*. Grand Rapids, Mich.: Zondervan, 1973

Love, Julian Price, *Laymans Bible Commentary, Vol. 25*. Richmond, Va.: John Knox Press, 1960

Ludwigson, R., *A Survey of Bible Prophecy*. Grand Rapids, Mich.: Zondervan, 1973

MacPherson, Dave, *The Unbelievable Pre-Trib Origin*. Kansas City, Mo.: Heart of America Bible Society, 1973

MacPherson, Norman S., *Tell It Like It Will Be*. Published by author, 7723 Robin Ave. N.E., Albuquerque, N.M., 1970

Manley, G. T., *The Return of Jesus Christ*. Downers Grove, Ill.: Inter-Varsity Press, 1972

McKeating, Henry, *God and the Future*. Valley Forge, Pa.: Judson Press, 1974

Morris, Leon, *New International Commentary on the New Testament* (1 and 2 Thessalonians), Grand Rapids, Mich.: Eerdmans, 1959

Mussner, Franz, *What Did Jesus Teach About the End of the World?* Ann Arbor, Mich.: Word of Life, 1974

Oosterwal, Gottfried, *Modern Messianic Movements*. Scottdale, Pa.: Herald Press, 1973

Payne, J. Barton, *Encyclopedia of Biblical Prophecy*. New York, N.Y.: Harper and Row, 1973

Ryrie, Charles Caldwell, *The Living End*. Old Tappan, N.J.: Revell, 1973

Schmithals, Walter, *The Apocalyptic Movement*. Nashville, Tenn.: Abingdon, 1975

Shank, Robert, *God's Tomorrow*. Springfield, Mo.: Westcott Publishers, 1975

Smith, J. B., *A Revelation of Jesus Christ*. Scottdale, Pa.: Herald Press, 1961

Studer, Gerald C., *After Death, What*. Scottdale, Pa.: Herald Press, 1976

Tenney, Merrill C., *Interpreting Revelation*. Grand Rapids, Mich.: Eerdmans, 1957

Travis, Stephen, *The Jesus Hope*. Downers Grove, Ill.: Inter-Varsity, 1976

Walvoord, John F., *The Blessed Hope and the Tribulation*. Grand Rapids, Mich.: Zondervan, 1976

Wenger, John C., *Introduction to Theology*. Scottdale, Pa.: Herald Press, 1954

Werner, Elert, *Last Things*. St. Louis, Mo.: Concordia, 1974

White, John Wesley, *Re-Entry*. Grand Rapids, Mich.: Zondervan, 1971

Wood, Leon J., *The Bible and Future Events*. Grand Rapids: Zondervan, 1973

INDEX OF SCRIPTURE CITED

OLD TESTAMENT

204

NEW TESTAMENT

206